WINNING STRATEGIES

for Test Taking,
Grades 3–8

For Marcia Stein, Mike Kelly, and Roger Pothus,
whose love and encouragement nourish us on our life journeys.

WINNING STRATEGIES

for Test Taking,
Grades 3–8

A Practical Guide for Teaching Test Preparation

Linda Denstaedt,
Judy Cova Kelly,
and Kathleen Kryza

Skyhorse Publishing

Skyhorse Publishing books may be purchased in bulk at special discounts for sales promotion, corporate gifts, fund-raising, or educational purposes. Special editions can also be created to specifications. For details, contact the Special Sales Department, Skyhorse Publishing, 307 West 36th Street, 11th Floor, New York, NY 10018 or info@skyhorsepublishing.com.

Skyhorse® and Skyhorse Publishing® are registered trademarks of Skyhorse Publishing, Inc.®, a Delaware corporation.

Visit our website at www.skyhorsepublishing.com.

10 9 8 7 6 5 4 3 2 1

Library of Congress Cataloging-in-Publication Data

Denstaedt, Linda.
 Winning strategies for test taking, grades 3-8 : a practical guide to teaching test preparation / Linda Denstaedt, Judy Cova Kelly, and Kathleen Kryza.
    p. cm.
 Originally published: Thousand Oaks, Calif. : Corwin Press, c2009.
 Includes bibliographical references and index.
 ISBN 978-1-61608-564-3 (pbk. : alk. paper)
 1. Test-taking skills--Study and teaching (Elementary) 2. Test-taking skills--Study and teaching (Middle school) I. Kelly, Judy Cova. II. Kryza, Kathleen. III. Title.
 LB3060.57.D46 2012
 371.26--dc23
                              2011040873

Printed in China

Contents

Preface

Winners have simply formed the habit of doing things losers don't like to do.

—Albert Gray, Official of
the Prudential Insurance Company of America

In this age of high-stakes testing, teachers feel pressured to spend more and more valuable time preparing students to take tests and less and less time preparing students for life beyond school and tests. The problem is kids don't really care about tests! Today's students want to be inspired, challenged—they want to see a connection between what they are learning and their lives. When we focus on rote memorization of information over meaningful learning, more and more students do not see school as a place where they are learning information relevant to their lives. And we are losing them. According to Klem and Connell (2004), "By high school, as many as 40–60% of all students—urban, suburban and rural, are chronically disengaged from school" (p. 263). Clearly, teaching to a test or focusing a majority of teaching time on test taking is not working for students (or for teachers for that matter). But tests do have their place in the world of education. So how do we strike a balance between preparing students to be effective test takers with preparing them for the world of the 21st century?

We decided to write this book to help teachers find that balance. In our many years as educators, we've discovered that the methods teachers apply to test preparation make all the difference. So we designed this book to help teachers prepare students for tests *and* for life using methods that are engaging and meaningful for students in Grades 3 through 8. The goals of the book are to (1) inspire students by helping them see themselves as competent learners and confident test takers, (2) show teachers and students the important life skills that are inherent in learning to take tests, and (3) create an efficient three-week unit of study on test taking that allows teachers and students to deeply learn the skills and strategies needed for test taking so they can spend the rest of the year on other necessary and meaningful learning.

To inspire students to become confident test takers *and* lifelong learners, we teach them skills that they own, skills that genuinely transfer out of the classroom and skills that make a difference in their lives. "A key finding in the learning and transfer literature is that organizing information into a conceptual framework allows for greater 'transfer'; that is, it allows the student to apply what was learned in new situations and to learn related information more quickly" (National Research Council, 2000, p. 78). Transfer from school to everyday environments is the ultimate purpose of school-based learning.

Throughout the book, we ask teachers and students to reframe test taking by thinking about it as a sport or a game. Like sports and games, test taking requires learning a set of skills and employing a set of strategies to reach a final goal. These skills and strategies can be learned through practice, just as skills and strategies needed to play a sport or game are learned. When students see the connection between sports or games and test taking, it not only raises the appeal of test taking, but also helps connect the skills they are learning to their lives outside of school. Therefore, teaching test taking within the sport or game analogy creates a powerful conceptual framework to help students acquire and transfer the skills they need to succeed in and out of school.

To show students and teachers the important life skills that are inherent in learning to take tests, we studied and researched state tests from around the country. We analyzed the kind of thinking and responding that learners are expected to do on these tests. (See Figure P.1, "Characteristics of Standardized Tests.") Then we extrapolated the key metacognitive skills students need to acquire this kind of thinking and responding.

This allowed us to show students that learning important metacognitive skills will prepare them to be both good test takers and lifelong learners. For example, when teaching students to write to a prompt (a type of writing they probably will not use once they are done with school), teachers can suggest that there are powerful metacognitive skills embedded in learning to write to prompts. The ability to quickly and effectively frame, organize, and communicate thoughts is indeed a skill students will continue to use throughout life (in job interviews, at social events, even convincing their parents to let them stay overnight with their friend). Now students can see the connection between what we are asking them to do for the short term and how it will benefit them in the long term. Learning to take tests includes valuable life skills such as metacognitive self-talk, decision making, and formulating effective responses.

Figure P.1   Characteristics of Standardized Tests

Characteristics of Standardized Tests

- Tests sometimes crowd many words on a page.

- Questions always follow the selections.

- Multiple-choice test questions are sometimes written in very formal English.

- Multiple-choice test questions may ask about a similar concept in different ways.

- Multiple-choice answers sometimes include distracters that draw attention away from the correct answer.

Finally, we designed the book as a unit of study—a practical step-by-step guide to make it easy and enjoyable for both students and teachers to prepare for taking tests. Each chapter begins with a game target that highlights what students will *understand, know,* and be *able to do* once they complete each part of the unit. This serves as a guide and a focus for the teacher and the students. Each chapter also includes detailed instructional steps for explicitly teaching, modeling, and scaffolding instruction of the outlined understandings and skills so that students actually own them and can transfer them into practical use after they leave school. The book contains many strategies, samples, and forms in easy-to-use table formats. Additional reproducible forms can be downloaded from our website, www.kathleenkryza.com.

The clear message we want to impart in this book is that preparing students to take tests is important, but testing should not be a teacher's primary means of assessing and learning in the classroom. We designed our book to allow teachers to do a deep two- to three-week study on test taking and then be free the rest of the year to engage and inspire students with learning that is essential to their lives. If teachers have deeply taught students test-taking skills and strategies, then prior to taking tests, they can remind students to apply the skills they know to the test-taking situation. It's important to note that traditional assessments such as tests should be balanced with performance-based assessments. These alternative assessments allow for student choice, for creativity, and for building the critical thinking and social skills they will need to compete in today's global workforce.

Can preparing students to take tests be a rich, meaningful, and professionally sound use of teachers' and students' valuable time? We think it all depends on how you decide to play the game!

The game's on—come join us!

Acknowledgments

We would especially like to thank Laura Schiller, who encouraged and collaborated with us in the early stages of this work. Also, we value our relationships with colleagues in the Oakland Writing Project, the Eastern Michigan Writing Project, and the National Writing Project, as well the teachers with whom we each work in Michigan and around the nation. We would also like to thank Lucy Calkins and coauthors Kate Montgomery, Beverly Falk, and Donna Santman for *A Teacher's Guide to Standardized Reading Tests: Knowledge Is Power,* which shifted our conversations in test preparation from test practice to genre study.

Linda would like to thank Lesley Banyky, Karen Gonzales, K. C. Leh, David Reschke, and a group of teacher researchers from Pine Knob Elementary and Sashabaw Elementary in Clarkston Community Schools in Clarkston, Michigan. Together they imagined, designed, and implemented units of study that engaged all learners in becoming successful readers, writers, and test takers. In addition, she thanks Shannon Moscovic and her students for opening their classroom for study, as well as the teachers from Oak Park Schools in Oak Park, Michigan. She also would like to thank her sons, Geoff and Scott; Laura Roop; Joseph Froslie; and her writing group for being her best teachers and thoughtful supporters.

Judy would like to thank Charlotte Woelmer, who collaborated on an early version of a test genre study. Also she would like to thank the teachers of Monroe Public Schools in Monroe, Michigan, in whose classrooms she began this work. In addition, she would like to thank the teachers of Eyler, Niedermeier, Ritter, and Sterling Elementary Schools in Airport Community Schools in Carleton, Michigan, and the teachers of Raisinville Elementary School of Monroe Public Schools in Monroe, Michigan: These teachers keep the conversation going.

Kathleen would like to thank Carol Ann Tomlinson, Grant Wiggins, and Jaye McTighe, master teachers whose ideas and teachings have deepened her thinking and inspired her work in helping teachers differentiate instruction and teach for meaning. She extends a loving thanks to Alicia

Duncan and Joy Stephens, the amazing educators, coauthors, and friends who provide love, laughter, and dreams on the journey to create a better world for children. Finally, she would like to thank the many dedicated teachers and administrators she has worked with across the country, whose willingness to take risks and venture onto new pedagogical paths continues to encourage her and remind her that together we can and will create the change we wish to see in the world.

We are fortunate to have Carol Chambers Collins as our editor; her vision enabled us to make this book a reality. In addition, we are grateful for the editorial direction of Brett Ory, and the production team of Veronica Stapleton and Claire Larson, who supported and advised us as we completed the book.

PUBLISHER'S ACKNOWLEDGMENTS

The publisher gratefully acknowledges the contributions of the following reviewers.

Dr. Deborah Alexander-Davis
Educational Consultant, Retired Elementary School Principal
Kingston Elementary School
Kingston, TN

Margaret Burkholder
Mathematics Instructor
K–12 International Academy
Herndon, VA

Susan Stone Kessler
Executive Principal
Hunters Lane High School
Metropolitan Nashville Public Schools
Nashville, TN

Kimberly Kyff
2007 Michigan Teacher of the Year
Jamieson Elementary/Middle School
Detroit, MI

Elizabeth Martin
Administrator/Educator
Baltimore, MD

Fredricka Reisman
Assistant Provost for Assessment and Evaluation
Drexel University
Philadelphia, PA

Joy Rose
High School Principal—Retired
Westerville, OH

Susan Stewart
Curriculum Consultant, Adjunct Professor
Ashland University
Massillon, OH

Patricia L. Waller
Past-President, National Association of Biology Teachers
Reston, VA

About the Authors

Linda Denstaedt has codirected the Oakland Writing Project since 2002. Prior to her work as an independent literacy consultant, Denstaedt taught ninth through twelfth grade English for 31 years. Denstaedt also taught creative writing, fifth grade, and physical education, and she was both the reading coordinator and the language arts coordinator for the Clarkston Community Schools at different points throughout her career. Since 1996, Denstaedt has authored texts for writing and reading in middle school and high school. Most recently, she coauthored *Going Places* and *On the Go,* texts for college composition.

Judy Cova Kelly is currently an independent literacy consultant with experience teaching elementary and higher education classes. Kelly has presented at national and statewide professional conferences on classroom structure, writer's workshops, reading comprehension instruction, and assessment training. For the Michigan Department of Education, Kelly sat on a committee to revise statewide grade-level content expectations. She has published articles on literacy in the *Language Arts Journal of Michigan* and *Michigan Reading Journal.* Kelly codirects the Monroe Writing Institute, which is a satellite of the Eastern Michigan Writing Project.

 **Kathleen Kryza** consults internationally for her company, Infinite Horizons, and also presents nationally for the Bureau of Education and Research and the National Council of Teachers of English. Kathleen has more than 20 years' experience in motivating and reaching children, educators, and others through her teaching, consulting, coaching, and writing. Her expertise is in working with students in special education, gifted education, alternative education, and multicultural education. Kathleen is co-author of two other Corwin books: *Inspiring Middle and Secondary Learners* and *Inspiring Elementary Learners.* She resides in Ann Arbor, Michigan, with her husband, Roger, and their "kids," Rennie (the dog) and Sasha (the cat).

Coaching Test Thinkers

1

If nothing else, children should leave school with a sense that if they act, and act strategically, they can accomplish their goals.

—Peter Johnston (2004, p. 29)

GAME STRATEGY FOR TEACHERS

Understand That . . .

- When students see learning as relevant and meaningful to their lives, they are more likely to transfer the skills to other areas.
- Learners can develop the sense and skills needed to be effective learners and test takers when teachers teach metacognitively and teach for transfer.
- The skills learned in test taking can be transferred to other settings.

Know

- Transfer
- Metacognition
- Scaffold
- Explicit instruction
- Think-alouds

Able to Do

- Explicitly teach strategies
- Talk metacognitively about thinking as students engage with tests
- Show how a strategy transfers from this application to a new application

THE HEAD START

As early as late July, chain stores and office suppliers begin stacking their shelves with school supplies. Notebooks sell for 79¢ and pocket folders for 10¢. Crowds of wise shoppers stock up, but most of these shoppers are teachers buying school supplies for their own students. Some participate in fan-out calling. If anyone sees a great sale, the calling chain goes into action. They want to be prepared. They know the value of a head start because, by October, it is too late. Those same notebooks will cost $2.99, and pocket folders will cost 79¢.

Likewise, every teacher wants to get a head start on test preparation. The dates for the state-mandated tests or districtwide achievement tests are on school calendars along with teacher conferences and holiday breaks. Every building or district has its own plan for test preparation. Getting a focused and effective head start may be the most important part of that plan.

Look at the challenges facing one teacher and 28 students. It is the end of the first week of school. Shannon, a third-grade teacher, has already created a great classroom community, partially assessed the reading, writing, and math skills of each of her students, established her reading and writing routines, and now she has to prepare her students for the state tests, which are given in October. To complicate matters, by state mandate, Shannon has only the first 14 days of school to show students the test or talk about how to take it. By law, she cannot mention the test or have test-related artifacts on her classroom walls for the 10 days prior to the test. Now pause and imagine 28 third graders who are not quite ready to give up sunshine and grassy days of play. In addition, imagine the range of reading abilities, attention spans, and emotional temperaments in that classroom. How can she develop confident and competent learners and, eventually, test takers? How can she pull out a state test and tell her squirming youngsters that now it is time to learn how to take a test?

What Shannon chooses to do is focus her test preparation on a few effective test-taking strategies and explicitly teach them so her students can use the strategies with increasing confidence, competence, and independence. She will also teach across the year knowing that her third graders will take the same state test next October in fourth grade. Teaching for transfer and independence are at the top of Shannon's planning list. Her plan is part of a grade-level plan that was designed by her building and is supported by her district.

If you are reading this book, you, like Shannon, are facing a state-mandated, high-stakes test at some point in your academic year. You are looking for solutions to the challenges you face as you prepare your students. You may be a single teacher or a group of colleagues in a book study. You may be a school improvement team looking for strategies and data to accomplish the goals in your strategic plan. In any case, you are ready to learn some powerful and meaningful ways to prepare students for taking tests.

THE TRUTH ABOUT TEST PREPARATION

Why do students study and prepare for tests? To get to the right answer! To pass the test! The more answers students get right, the higher the chance they will pass the test. However, students may not see it that simply. (We may not see it that simply either.) But that is what it is. Testing is the same as any game experience. When the buzzer rings at the end of the game, a score of 67–66 is still a winning score.

Some teachers might argue that it is not enough to just pass. And they would be right. It is not enough. These teachers see a score of 67–66 as barely winning, and it is barely winning, but it is winning. State tests

> **TIME-OUT**
>
> **Examine Your Test: What challenges will your students encounter on your state test?**
>
> Jot down a list of challenges your students may face. How do these challenges become decisions for your test-preparation instruction? Add a list of ways you, your grade-level team, building, or district are addressing these challenges.

connected to the No Child Left Behind Act put teachers and schools in a similar dilemma. They ask: How will I coach my struggling students to pass a test that is too difficult for them at this time in their educational lives? If your school or district needs to make annual yearly progress (AYP), passing is in the forefront of your mind. Quality teaching and learning form an effective strategy to ensure AYP; focused test preparation is their partner.

Your students can pass. Test-taking strategies empower all students. Confidence increases motivation to engage with a test. Increasing engagement can impact scores positively. In this way, passing a test is like playing a game, because it requires strategy and the determination to face each challenge as it emerges. James Paul Gee (2004) parallels decoding print to playing a game. He suggests that "A child or an adult is engaging in a 'game' whenever they are taking on a specific sort of identity defined by certain 'moves': that is, certain sorts of actions and interactions that define them as playing a certain sort of role" (p. 46). If we use this game metaphor, we understand as students take up the role of test taker, they are learning ways to act in the test setting and strategies to interact with the test. Test taking is not a game; it is serious business. But like a game, it has legal moves and effective strategies. Students can develop the skills and strategies they need to feel competent and confident and not give up. From this perspective, we remind students that tests provide a single snapshot of their abilities on a given day; they do not tell their whole story as learners. We also want to help them see that in learning to take tests they are developing an academic skill, but they are also gaining life knowledge and learning important procedures. Using the practices in this book, we can help students see a connection between the skills they learn in test taking and the skills they will need in life.

This chapter addresses some ideas and strategies to help you get started and to help you build a mindset for making test preparation an engaging and meaningful experience for your students as well as yourselves.

Students who enter the test-taking setting with prior knowledge of how the test works will score significantly higher than students who don't know the test. So it's important for teachers who are preparing students for these tests to have knowledge of the test, its parts, the various demands, and the expectations. Think of the test as a genre like poetry or a textbook. A reader who understands how stanzas and line breaks work will find poetry more accessible. Likewise, a reader who understands how the headings, subheadings, and other textbook features work will find a textbook more accessible. Like any genre, tests are written by test writers who adhere to the expectations of the test genre. If students know how the test genre works, they can take the test more effectively. It seems the best way to learn about tests is to become a student of the test, researching the test content, format, and types of questions or responses and applying strategies to manage these elements.

TEACHING FOR UNDERSTANDING

Teaching for independent performance may be at the heart of all teaching and learning, but it is the key to developing test sense. Here teachers preparing children for a test are like the coach who uses language in conscious ways to name the thinking, processes, techniques, and plans players will use when they are in the midst of the game and alone on the court. The coach knows the player needs his own internal voice to notice and name the action on court and make split-second decisions. Where does the player get this internal voice? The list is long: the coach, other experienced players, time-outs during the game, watching and discussing game videos, and studying professional players. The coach knows becoming an independent player requires learning how to notice and name the actions occurring in a game in order to quickly retrieve the strategies to manage the action. The coach teaches the strategies, but also the self-assessing moment. The goal is modeling and practicing in situations to build the internal voice. As a result, the player becomes adept at asking a series of questions that enable her response: What do I see? What am I expected to do? How is this like or different from other experiences? What strategy do I know to respond effectively? How will I use or adjust this strategy?

Less is more. Teaching for an effective internal voice requires focus. A focused test-preparation unit with a few instructional practices and a few explicit strategies will translate to test success. The essential instructional practices teachers need to use to develop metacognitive learning that transfer into an internal voice for test success are explicit instruction, scaffolding, modeling, and think-alouds.

Teaching for understanding and transfer is essential to prepare students for a test

> **TIME-OUT**
>
> **Examine Your Test: How is the test organized and scored?**
>
> Take the test yourself. Become knowledgeable about how the test is constructed and how it is scored. Identify the parts of the test, the numbers and types of questions, and how those questions will be scored. For example, the writing portions of a test will be scored by an adult reader who is looking for specific traits of writing and specific kinds of evidence of thinking. In Chapters 4 and 5, we show you how to study those traits and have students practice test writing, which is its own unique genre of writing.
>
> Studying and analyzing the test with colleagues before you study the test with your students will direct and focus your teaching.

and to build confident performance in a test setting. In addition, teaching for understanding and transfer develops competent and confident learners who will apply prior learning to a variety of settings and contexts in school and in life. Learning with understanding engages students in active learning, encourages transfer of knowledge, and empowers students.

Transfer

Transfer occurs when students consciously use the strategies and skills they have learned in one setting to perform a task in a new setting. This sounds simple, and it might be for many physical and procedural tasks. If someone shows you how to hit a softball, most likely you can transfer that physical knowledge to hitting a baseball. The ball size and the speed of the pitch may make the task a bit harder, but the task is essentially the same, so you are able to transfer the skill. The National Research Council (2000) lists factors that enable the transfer of learning. To make test preparation effective, keep in mind a few key factors: learning is an active process focused on understanding; memorizing facts and "one-shot" exposures to information does not promote transfer; knowing "when, where, why and how to use knowledge" is essential to solving problems; and deliberate monitoring during practice develops evaluation of current understanding in order to develop flexible and adaptive use (p. 236).

Think about your own reading. As effective readers, you transfer knowledge every time you pick up a text. You integrate a complex series of skills and strategies to engage with the text. For example, you probably scan the text and identify the genre. If it is a science textbook, you know that textbook is harder to read because it is written in a formal style and contains difficult and technical vocabulary. You know to slow down and reread this kind of text. You know that the author will put this vocabulary in boldface and the definition of these boldfaced words will be in the paragraph. You also know textbooks have headings and subheadings that name the focus of the information. You rely on these aids because you know there will be questions at the end of the chapter, and you have learned that the boldface and headings will help you skim for the answers to these questions. Plus you know that important information is in the graphs, tables, maps, and illustrations. You are a successful textbook reader because you transfer this knowledge and use it to read your social studies, math, or English textbook. Unfortunately, struggling readers do not use and transfer skills like this unless a teaching coach has explicitly taught them to do so.

> **Students transfer knowledge of**
>
> **Procedures** to manage a task effectively and efficiently
>
> **Skills** to decode and comprehend a text or use mathematical concepts and formulas
>
> **Strategies** for questioning, clarifying, summarizing, elaborating, identifying, or monitoring
>
> **Processes** that enable generating, revising, or problem solving

Similarly, if students are to become successful test takers, they will need to transfer knowledge learned across a school year or accumulated over several years of school to a test setting. They may be asked to read and comprehend a passage and then answer multiple-choice questions. As a result, they must know how to use a series of cognitive skills and strategies that require conscious thinking and decision making as well as the procedural knowledge of reading the questions, matching the question with the blank on the answer sheet, and filling in blanks without smudging the marks.

The day of the test, your students will face unfamiliar reading, but if you have taught them well, the format of the test will be familiar, and they will transfer the skills and strategies taught to this new setting. They will know what is expected of them.

Therefore, teaching students to approach test taking with a level of game sense makes a difference. What is game sense? It is the ability to predict an outcome and develop or adapt strategies to determine a goal, a course of action, and a process for achieving that goal. Game sense requires the player to assess performance and adjust the course of action in the moment of playing. Game sense comes from being coached before the game by an expert who has played the game and understands the challenges of the game. This coaching focuses on the ability of the player to transfer knowledge and processes from the practice setting to the game setting. The player is, after all, alone in the game setting and dependent on the abilities learned in the practice setting. Game sense is test sense.

Coach students to have test sense by explicitly teaching them the skills, procedures, strategies, and processes that good test takers use. Only through explicit instruction will students own and be able to transfer necessary skills to the test-taking situation.

Explicit Instruction

Instruction focused with the end in mind has explicit goals. Teachers explicitly state the target for the thinking and actions students will acquire. Each lesson contains an explicit teaching point that students enact. A single teaching point is most effective since students are able to understand and use this single strategy immediately. Each lesson offers step-by-step procedures that unpack and name what students need to understand, know, and do. Immediate use and success enables students to integrate that lesson into their test-sense repertoire. Each lesson offers teachers ways to think aloud the thought processes that successful learners use. Organized by an instructional scaffold, students feel safe and successful as they face often-challenging skills. Explicit teaching of test-taking skills creates the metacognitive voice students use to discern and process the demands of a test.

In Figure 1.1, the teacher names the strategy the students will enact as well as the purpose and process for using the strategy. In this sample lesson, the strategies are in boldface and the purpose and process are labeled.

Metacognition

Metacognition is the internal voice students and teachers both use to monitor their thinking. Metacognition enables students to gradually gain confidence as they monitor their own sense making, strategy use, and self-assessment. They can identify their strengths as well as their weaknesses, set goals, and transfer learning (National Research Council, 2000, pp. 235–237).

Learning to transfer skills, strategies, knowledge, and processes to new settings is the goal of any instruction. Metacognitive activities

Figure 1.1   Example of Explicit Instruction: A Single Teaching Point

Connects today's lesson with previous learning	Yesterday we examined the **essay question and identified key words** in the question to help you focus your writing and identify the type of writing you are expected to use in your response. Together, we determined this essay question is expecting you to write a personal narrative to illustrate the idea that lessons you learned can change the way you see something. **Today I will show you one strategy to generate a personal narrative in order to respond to this test question** about learning a lesson. **The strategy is to write about a person that is important to you.** Using a person that is important helps you identify several stories. Begin by selecting a person, then list stories that show how that person taught you a specific lesson. This strategy of writing about a person that is important will work with this test question and other questions that are similar to this one.
States purpose for this strategy	
Identifies today's strategy lesson	
States purpose and process for today's strategy lesson	

encourage students to act in certain ways and take on an identity as a knower and user of strategies and self-regulation. It also encourages them to become aware of their self-talk. A positive internal voice in which students intentionally manage their own learning will impact learning and performance in and out of school. However, it may be the primary goal for successful test taking.

Some students will face reading or writing beyond their current independent level. You have probably watched these students as they rushed through the test or put their head down without finishing. If students enter the test setting with negative self-talk, then the test is a difficult experience, proving once again the students' incompetence. Knowledge about learning and what is being learned, as well as experience with the task, plays a role in developing a metacognitive internal voice. This self-regulatory voice develops over time (National Research Council, 2000, pp. 97–98). Imagine changing that internal voice so your students have an encouraging internal partner, providing the stamina to stay with a difficult task as they apply the strategies they have learned. Although some of your students may not pass the test, metacognition may help them to see themselves as intentional and on some level successful.

Moving From Negative Self-Talk to Metacognition

One morning I observed a teacher as she explained the reading strategy the students would use to mark up a short passage and find the main idea. Students would use this strategy in a few months for a state test. As I listened, my attention was drawn to Matt sitting in the back of the class. Slumped in his chair, his eyes politely looked at the teacher, but his head occasionally shook as if he were saying, "No." After the brief lesson, I walked up to him, described what I saw, and asked, "What is your head saying?" Matt replied, "I'm afraid to read. I can't read."

However, he agreed to read a paragraph aloud with me. I listened to him read slowly, word by word. He self-corrected, reread, and connected the parts of words. He consciously responded to the punctuation as he painstakingly read five sentences with 100% accuracy. Immediately, I complimented the way he read with a high degree of accuracy. I added that it was obvious that he used a variety of strategies, and I listed them. Matt let out an audible sigh of relief. I asked how he learned those strategies. He couldn't remember. I asked if he remembered or understood what he read. He replied, "I never remember what I read." I asked what he thinks about when he reads. He said, "Nothing."

I did not believe his last statement. I did believe he may not be aware of the complex thinking he uses to read. I imagined Matt's internal voice reinforced his fear of failure. He read slowly because he was telling himself that he might not get the next word right. He anticipated failure even as he was succeeding. He was not aware of the sophisticated combination of strategies he used to read. In Matt's mind, he approached every page of words empty-handed. As a result, he hated reading and writing. He also hated tests, especially timed tests.

Together we altered the assignment. He would continue his slow reading process that has helped him read so effectively. He would still read and underline sentences that stated the main idea. However, he would read only half of the assignment so he could make time to pay attention to his thinking. I asked him how he thought he might do this. He explained that he would circle the headings that separated the four parts of the reading and find one sentence in each section because often the main idea is in one sentence. I asked him where in the section he expected to find that sentence. He was not sure, but he guessed at the beginning or end. He knew that he could read at least two sections in the time allowed. He decided that he would read the first two, but maybe he could do the others if he focused his reading.

(Continued)

(Continued)

At this point, it seemed clear that Matt's fear of reading made him unable to recognize what he knew how to do.

I suggested that he pause to make sense at the end of each paragraph and pause again at the end of a section. He might even reread to find the one sentence. He nodded in agreement—his approach was clear. Then I added, "This time, instead of worrying about getting all the words right, pay attention to what you do as you read and if this approach helped. When you finish, we will talk about your findings."

I thought Matt's negative self-image as a reader needs to be replaced with a positive, metacognitive voice. When I returned, Matt had almost completed the assignment using his approach. I asked, "So what did you notice as you read?" He remarked that this article was easier than he first thought; and although he was not a good reader, it helped to slow down and worry less. He added that his approach worked. He was right about circling headings and finding one sentence that stated the main idea. This one brief conference did not magically change Matt's opinion of himself as a reader, create an internal voice that helped him confidently monitor his comprehension, or translate him into a metacognitive learner. However, this conference could be the first step in a year-long journey to focus his attention from reading words to understanding what he did as he read—to become aware and monitor his thinking.

Think-Alouds

One of the most powerful ways to teach students to be metacognitive test takers is to let them see inside the minds of effective test takers. Think-alouds make a teacher's thinking public; it lets students see the test expert's internal, metacognitive voice as it manages each test challenge. This modeling demonstrates how an expert automatically retrieves information to solve problems or address challenges (National Research Council, 2000, pp. 237–238) As a result, thinking aloud requires that the teachers slow down and analyze how they employ strategies effectively.

Equally important is providing the opportunity for students to think aloud. Turn-and-talk partnerships provide time for students to try out the thinking a teacher previously modeled. This moment of rehearsal ensures that all students speak aloud their thoughts. At first, turning and talking is unfamiliar or uncomfortable, but as teachers pair explicit teaching with metacognitive thinking aloud, student conversations improve in quality.

Explicitly teaching critical listening also improves conversation quality. After students talk, ask them to explain what their partner said rather than what they themselves said. This simple act of *saying back* the words and thoughts of the partner encourages students to both listen carefully and speak thoughtfully. Later ask students to *talk back* by stating their thoughts or *add on* by extending the thoughts of another student (Calkins, 2001).

Thinking aloud is crucial when test questions require students to make inferences. Inferring combines prior knowledge with information from the text. In a think-aloud, teachers notice and identify important details in a test passage. Then they use prior knowledge to recognize relationships and determine the meaning and purpose of test passages. Figure 1.2 illustrates how an expert test reader thinks aloud as he constructs meaning from a test question. Thinking aloud is especially important in a test setting when time is a factor.

Figure 1.2   Think-Aloud Model

Text	Teacher Think-Aloud
The following table shows the cost of tickets for a play	I notice that this table shows the cost of tickets at a glance. It shows the cost of 1, 2 or 3 tickets. Hmmm . . . it does not show the cost of 4 or 5 tickets.
Play Tickets table:	The question asks me to figure out the cost of 5 tickets. That is why the question mark is in the table, but the price of 4 tickets is blank, so I guess I don't have to figure that amount out.

Play Tickets	
1	$3.50
2	$7.00
3	$10.50
4	
5	?

If the cost of each ticket is the same, what will the total cost of 5 tickets be?

    A. $14.00
    B. $14.50
    C. $17.00
    D. $17.50

So what are the important pieces of information in the table that will help me figure out the cost of 5 tickets?

I know the price of 3 tickets is $10.50. I need to add the price of 2 tickets to it to determine the price of 5 tickets. I can do this by adding one ticket at a time like the table does it. But the table also shows the price of 2 tickets is $7.00. So if I add $10.50 and $7.00, I will have the price of 5 tickets.

Five tickets will be $17.50. So "D" is the correct answer. Now before I go on, let me double check by adding one ticket at a time. Yes, I am sure I have that right! Next problem.

From *Florida Comprehensive Assessment Test: Sunshine State Standards.* Grade 4. Released October 2005.

Although this math problem is quite simple for many students, the thinking involved to solve it is not. It requires a student to notice the important information in the question and the table to identify the math work required and to determine the answer. For some students, this thinking is automatic. For other students, this thinking must be explicitly taught. The more consciously students think, the more consciously they apply their knowledge of a text as well as math concepts and processes to the next new and different math problem.

This is the challenge and the goal of teaching for understanding. Teachers who think aloud for their students model their own thinking as a knowledgeable adult and expert reader. They ask their students to apprentice themselves into thinking in a similar way through turning and talking. They also know that everyone thinks in a slightly different way, so they focus their think-alouds on specific strategies and processes that are universal and can be used by each learner in a test or be transferred to other settings as well.

Scaffold

The teacher who coaches learning takes a different position in the classroom. This classroom functions around talking and critical listening. The classroom community includes the teacher, the student learner, and other student learners of varying abilities. All community participants actually coach each other's attempts at learning a skill or strategy as they interact and apply that strategy.

Scaffolding instruction of test taking means teaching students in small, safe steps that build and encourage success. Think of a lesson as flight of stairs. In each lesson, students take small steps that add up to confident use of a strategy. First, the teacher explicitly states the teaching point of the lesson. Then, most often, he demonstrates and thinks aloud to model or show students the concept, strategy, or process he uses and they will use. Second, the students try the teaching point with a partner. As they think aloud together, they understand the lesson and how to enact it. Third, students try the strategy on their own in independent work. Finally, the teacher asks the

> **TIME-OUT**
>
> **How do I think
> when I take a test?**
>
> Select a test question from your state test. With a partner, think aloud how you read the question and how you selected an answer. Have your partner jot notes to capture your thinking. Review the notes and discuss the following questions.
>
> 1. What did you do in order to think aloud?
>
> 2. Was your thinking aloud effective? What made it clear for a student? What needs clarification?

students to share their work with a partner. Sharing demands that students name and explain what they learned and how they applied it. It also allows for a partner to interact and adjust the thinking or work. In this interaction, getting the right-answer is not as important as knowing how to get the next-answer using the same concept, strategy, or process. This final step transfers the learning into the students' internal, metacognitive voice. Scaffolding instruction enables students to approximate learning as they enact, gain confidence with, and eventually own their own test sense.

DESIGNING THE UNIT AND LESSON ORGANIZATION

A focused test preparation unit may require two to three weeks of classroom instruction prior to the test. By controlling test preparation to a few weeks, teachers engage students in the quality instruction necessary to accelerate learning and create strategic and independent thinkers. After examining your state's test, review and select the strategies that best fit the demands of your state test.

Designing the Unit

Chapters 2 through 5 provide the basic strategies needed for successful test sense in reading, question answering, constructive response, and prompt writing. Review and select the strategies that fit your test.

Each chapter opens with a summary box stating the big ideas in the chapter: what your students will understand, know, and be able to do to respond to the demands of your state test and test setting. These big ideas are explored through analysis of a variety of tests across the nation. The body of each chapter lists key strategies and demonstrates how to use and create a lesson to teach each strategy. For each specific strategy, the following information is provided.

1. Models of questions or prompts from several state tests and commentary to illustrate how this strategy works. This helps you understand the strategy as well as analyze questions to apply the strategy to your test.

2. Step-by-step game plans that walk you through each lesson.

3. Self-assessment moments for you and your students.

4. Text boxes that indicate connections students can make to other content or real life so they can see that test-taking strategies work in other settings.

Lesson Organization

The structure of each lesson or Game Plan Practice Session explicitly teaches a strategy, providing multiple opportunities to rehearse and practice the strategy in a whole group setting, partnership conversations, and self-monitored practice. Each lesson closes with a teacher assessment, student self-assessment, and goal setting to encourage metacognitive thinking and transfer to the test setting. The teacher also charts the teaching point or game strategy taught. Charting creates a public reminder of the teaching points and enables students to read, remember, and use the strategies taught today in future practice with the test or future lessons throughout the year. A daily lesson scaffold is explained in Figure 1.3, Lesson Scaffold.

Figure 1.3   Lesson Scaffold

Game Plan Practice Session

Parts of Lesson	Purpose of Parts	Method of Support
Equipment	Materials needed to implement the lesson	Each state has a Web site created by the Department of Education. Released tests and other materials are available for teacher study and use with test preparation lessons.
Connection	Teacher states the teaching point of a previous lesson and how it is connected to today's teaching point.	• Connects the lessons • Creates a relationship
Game strategy: Teaching point	Teacher demonstrates or guides students through the application of the teaching point: skill, strategy, or process.	• States explicitly the teaching point • Demonstrates how to use the information, process, skill, or strategy • Explains why the teaching point is important to know
Skill practice: Try it in partnerships	Students work in partnerships to try the skill, strategy, or process demonstrated by the teacher.	• Rehearses skill, strategy, or process before independent practice • Listens to another student try a skill, strategy, or process • Gains understanding of how and why this teaching point is useful and effective

Parts of Lesson	Purpose of Parts	Method of Support
Own it: Independent practice	Individual students use the lesson.	• Practices the skill, strategy, or process • Monitors and assesses application of lesson
Huddle: Assess and reflect	Students monitor and assess their personal thinking and work through focused, metacognitive conversations in pairs or as a whole class.	• Prepares work to present to others • Listens critically to the work of others to understand how they accomplished the task • Reflects on similarities and differences in application of the lesson • Self-assesses today's performance • Sets goals for future use or ways to adjust the skill, strategy, or process for future use
Review game strategy: Link	Teacher rephrases the teaching point and its application to today's work and future work.	• Names the teaching point and explains it again to adjust for or address students' confusions or successes • Connects the lessons to today's work and future work

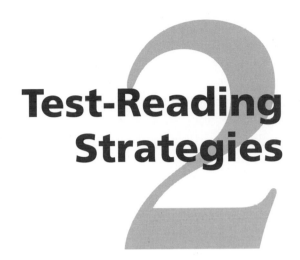

Test-Reading Strategies

So our goal when we work with teachers and students in classrooms is to explicitly teach a repertoire of thinking strategies that are used to further the cause of understanding and engagement.

—Harvey and Goudvis (2007, p. 14)

GAME STRATEGY FOR STUDENTS

Understand That . . .

- When reading a test, readers use the same effective reading strategies they use all the time, but they use them more intentionally for test purposes.

Know

- Effective test-reading strategies

Able to Do

- Independently utilize the reading strategies taught throughout the school year while reading a test
- Independently use reading strategies to read expository and narrative texts in a test setting

SETTING A PURPOSE

The most important reason to read during a test is to get the answers correct, just like the reason to play a game is to score well. Because this is the purpose, test readers have to be engaged and alert the entire time they are reading the test. Test readers need to utilize comprehension strategies while using their interacting voices. They must create sensory images, infer, activate schema, synthesize, question, determine importance, and monitor comprehension.

If reading is thinking, teach your students what kind of thinking they might do while reading a test. There are a few strategies to teach students that will enhance their strategic reading and thinking on a test, but first discuss the purpose for reading on the test—getting the answers right. Then help students understand how to remain engaged with the text. Test reading requires a heightened alertness that other reading does not.

The following strategies not only enable students to engage with the text, they also teach them what to focus on while reading. Test takers try to cram in as much information as possible as they read because that information may be asked about in the questions they encounter (Calkins, Montgomery, Falk, & Santman, 1998). To be efficient, they need to know how to distinguish the important from unimportant information.

GAME STRATEGY: INTERACTING AND DISTRACTING VOICES

Telling students that reading is thinking is not enough. Make your thinking visible to your students for them to truly understand what this means. While reading a test, your students must be engaged, thinking readers.

In her book *I Read It, But I Don't Get It*, Chris Tovani (2000) describes the three voices in readers' heads as they read: the *reciting*, the *interacting*, and the *distracting*. The reciting voice is the voice they hear reading the words of the text. The interacting voice is the voice that talks back to the text, making connections, inferences, and so forth. The distracting voice is the voice that takes readers away from the reading; for example, they may begin to think about lunch or what they are doing that evening, rather than the text.

It is important to control the distracting voice and enhance the interacting one. All readers deal with these voices. Many readers find their interacting voices are loud and clear when reading fiction. They enter into the story, and the present world no longer exists. This may not be the case when they read professional or technical materials. They struggle to keep their distracting voices quiet and interacting voices engaged; because of this, it is more likely readers become tired and distracted while reading professional or technical books. They battle to stay focused.

Talk to students about this struggle. Let them know that, even though you are a good reader, you still work to manage these voices. All readers go through this.

When readers become distracted, they decide if they will go back and reread or go on reading. This decision depends upon their purpose and what they are reading. If they are studying a professional document they want to share with others, they reread to be sure they have a clear, thorough understanding. If they are reading a piece of fiction and don't think what they missed is important, they go on. All of this happens instantaneously and unconsciously. Pay attention to your thinking while reading and notice if you become distracted.

Figure 2.1 depicts some thoughts engaged readers might have using their interactive voices while reading a text. These thoughts are in direct response to the text and assist readers to comprehend what is read. Some of the comprehension strategies listed above are among the interactions. Also portrayed in Figure 2.1 is a *problem-solver voice*. Imagine readers who come across unknown words and an unidentified first-person narrator and look at these difficulties as problems to solve, not indicators of defeat or self-deficiencies. Perhaps these readers would sound like this example.

Figure 2.1   Engaged Voice Samples

Text	Interacting Voice	Problem-Solver Voice
Bob's Market		
It was a usual Saturday. But sometimes important lessons happen on <u>ordinary</u> days. Betty, Connie, Kim, and I went to Bob's	I wonder what the lesson will be.	What is this word (ordinary)? I wonder if it is important to the whole story. I'll keep reading and see if I can figure it out later.
Market for penny candy. Bob always teased me about being short, and I always <u>ignored</u> him. But everyone else laughed.	What is penny candy? I never saw candy that cost a penny.	Hmm . . . I am not sure of this word (ignored) either. It has something to do with being teased.
After picking our candy, we went around the corner into the alley along the back of the market toward the railroad tracks and the woods between our neighborhood and the high school.	I can imagine this part clearly—the alley with garbage cans that probably stink, railroad tracks with the big metal rails, and the woods with lots of trees.	

(Continued)

Figure 2.1 (Continued)

Text	Interacting Voice	Problem-Solver Voice
Connie noticed the sheet of glass. The corner was broken, and it leaned against the trash bins. Betty said, "We should break it."	What is a sheet of glass?	
"Yeah, great idea. Me first," Kim and Connie said together.	I bet the owner catches them.	
Then they threw a handful of pebbles. Nothing happened. Betty threw two large rocks.		
Nothing happened. Then I picked up a huge <u>boulder.</u> I stood right next to the glass and threw the		I am not sure what a boulder is, but it must be bigger than what the other kids threw.
rock down. The glass broke with a loud crash.	This person wants to prove—Hey I don't know if the narrator is a boy or girl or his name.	
Almost <u>immediately,</u> Betty, Connie, and Kim cheered.		Oh boy! I don't know this word (immediately), but it looks like immediate. I wonder if it means the same thing.
And Bob slammed the screen door at the back of the market. We looked at Bob <u>simultaneously.</u> Connie yelled, "Run!" And everyone ran, including me. At the end of the alley, I stopped. Why had I run away? What was I thinking?	I was right. Here comes Bob.	What does this mean (simultaneously)? I have no idea, but I get the story. These kids broke some glass and they are going to get into trouble so I must be doing okay reading it.
We rounded the corner at the end of the block, and Betty kept telling how I found the biggest rock, how I threw the hardest, and the best, how I broke the window. Kim just stared at me, and I knew that she would tell Mom when we got home. She always told. I didn't care about any of that. I could only think of Bob.		

Text	Interacting Voice	Problem-Solver Voice
"I'm going back. We have to turn ourselves in. He knows us," I said.		
"No way. He doesn't know me," Betty said.		
"Me either."		
"I didn't do anything," said Kim.		
"Well, he knows me, and I broke the window, and I have to go back."		
"Well, I'm not."		
"See ya at school."		
"I'm going home and tell Mom," Kim said.	Oh, I didn't realize Kim was this person's sister. I still don't know if it is a girl or a boy. I wonder what the mom will say. Mine would be mad. This kid is pretty brave; I am not sure I would have gone back alone.	
I walked back to Bob's alone. He was waiting behind the counter. There was no smile on his face. I walked straight up to the counter and apologized. He didn't yell. He handed me a broom.		
For the next week, I swept floors and carried out trash after school. To be honest, I		
enjoyed it. I knew I was wrong, and it was better to face my mistake and make it right. It was a good lesson to learn at 10 years old.	Oh, I see. The lesson must be to face up to your mistakes.	

There are three different ways readers might become distracted while reading. Examples of all three distracting voices are shown in Figure 2.2. One starts off as a connection, but veers off into an extended memory that takes the reader away from the text. This is a *wandering voice*. When reading the first wandering voice example in Figure 2.2, picture the reader's eyes traveling down the page while thinking about the memory of visiting Falzone's Drugstore. While the initial thought is a connection and may enhance meaning, the continued thought is not about what is happening in the text and acts as a distraction.

Another type of distraction is the negative self-talk some readers do when they encounter difficulty while reading. They interpret these difficulties as self-deficits rather than problems to solve. The *I can't do it voice* usually prevents a reader from even trying to go on. These readers don't understand *all* readers encounter difficulties. The issue is not whether they have difficulties reading or not; the issue is what readers do when they encounter difficulties. In the first example of the I can't do it voice, the reader quickly starts to use negative self-talk because he comes to words with which he is not familiar. Refer back to the problem-solver voice in Figure 2.1 for a contrast to the I can't do it voice.

The third type of distraction has no connection to the text. It is based solely in the reader's life. The *disconnected voice* may be a reaction to the reader's environment, such as a sound, and it pulls the reader away from the text. As in the disconnected voice example below, readers might be hungry and begin to think about the next meal, or they are excited about an upcoming sporting event and think about that rather than the text.

It is important to find out what distracts your students and how they pull themselves back to the text. What signals them that they are not thinking about what they are reading? How do they decide if they must reread or go on?

If you combined all of the interacting and distracting examples given, you would have a more complete example of the varied thinking readers do while reading. No one is totally engaged or totally disengaged.

TIME-OUT

What internal voices do I use when I read a test passage?

Select a passage from your state test. As you read it, jot down notes in the margin to document the voices you use: interacting voice, problem-solving voice, wandering voice, I can't do it voice, or disconnected voice. Compare your thinking with a partner.

1. **Which voices were you aware of?**

2. **How did you turn off the distracting voices and engage the interacting voices?**

Figure 2.2   Distracting Voice Samples

Text	Wandering Voice	I Can't Do It Voice	Disconnected Voice
Bob's Market			
It was a usual Saturday. But sometimes			
important lessons happen on <u>ordinary</u> days.		It's the second sentence and already I do not know a word (ordinary). I probably won't be able to read this.	
Betty, Connie, Kim, and I went to Bob's Market for penny candy. Bob always teased	I loved going to Falzone's Drugstore. They had all kinds of candy and a snack bar where you could buy flavored Cokes.		

Text	Wandering Voice	I Can't Do It Voice	Disconnected Voice
	Every Saturday when I got my allowance, I ran to buy the latest comic books. I loved looking at their jewelry and watches. The trays went around like they were on a Ferris wheel. I would stand there until someone told me I had to leave.		
me about being short, and I always <u>ignored</u> him. But everyone else laughed.		Here's another word (ignored) I do not know. Why do writers use such big words?	
After picking our candy, we went around the corner into the alley along the back of the market toward the railroad tracks and the woods between our neighborhood and the high school.			My stomach is growling. I wonder what we are having for lunch today.
Connie noticed the sheet of glass. The corner was broken, and it leaned against the			
trash bins. Betty said, "We should break it."			
"Yeah, great idea. Me first," Kim and Connie said together.			What time is it? This class will never end. I am starving! I think it is pizza day today. I hope it is better than last week when they burned it. I had to force myself to eat it because I was so hungry. The lunch lady did not even
Then they threw a handful of pebbles. Nothing happened.			

(Continued)

Figure 2.2 (Continued)

Text	Wandering Voice	I Can't Do It Voice	Disconnected Voice
Betty threw two large rocks. Nothing happened. Then I			respond to me when I complained and asked for a new piece. What a crab! I bet she wouldn't eat it.
picked up a huge boulder. I stood right next to the glass and threw the rock down. The glass broke with a loud crash.		Oh brother. I don't know this word (boulder). I thought maybe I could read this, but I don't think so. Maybe I am not smart enough to read this.	
Almost immediately, Betty, Connie, and Kim cheered. And Bob slammed the screen door at the back of the market. We looked at Bob simultaneously. Connie yelled, "Run!" And everyone ran, including me. At the end of the alley, I stopped. Why had I run away? What was I thinking?		Here are more words I do not know (immediately and simultaneously.) This story is stupid. I don't even know who is telling the story. I quit.	
We rounded the corner at the end of the block, and Betty kept telling how I found the biggest rock, how I threw the hardest, and the best, how I broke the window. Kim just stared at me, and I knew that she would			
tell Mom when we got home. She always told. I didn't care about any of that. I could only think of Bob.			I am so mad at my mom for not driving me to school today and I had to walk. I hate walking to school alone. Everyone gets

Text	Wandering Voice	I Can't Do It Voice	Disconnected Voice
"I'm going back. We have to turn ourselves in. He knows us," I said.			a ride. It is so boring. Not only that, I ended up being late for school. The teacher was all over me as soon as I hit the door for being late again.
"No way. He doesn't know me," Betty said. "Me either." "I didn't do anything," said Kim. "Well, he knows me, and I broke the window, and I have to go back." "Well, I'm not." "See ya at school." "I'm going home and tell Mom," Kim said. I walked back to Bob's alone. He was waiting behind the counter. There was no smile on his face. I walked straight up to the counter and apologized. He didn't yell. He just handed me a broom. For the next week I swept floors and carried out trash after school. To be honest, I enjoyed it. I knew I was wrong, and it was better to face my mistake and make it right. It was a good lesson to learn at 10 years old.	Once when I was at my cousin's house, I broke a piece to his Cootie game. He went to get us some pop. He told me not to play with the game until he returned. I tried to wait but I couldn't. I picked up one of the antennae and tried to put it into the hole, but it would not fit so I jammed it in as hard as I could, and it snapped in half. I didn't know what to do, so I quickly hid it back in the box and grabbed another piece. I never told him I broke the piece and he didn't notice it until later when he was playing with my brother. He started yelling, but I still didn't say anything.		

Game Plan Practice Session

Interacting and Distracting Voices

Equipment	• Released test passages or content area textbook • Optional transparencies of interacting and distracting voices • Game plan books • Chart paper and markers or transparency of the strategies
Connection	Students, the strategies you will learn over our next course of study will change how you take and think about tests. It is like you just found the play book for the opposing team. You will keep track of these strategies in these game plan books. I will refer to these strategies as game strategies and will coach you to success. Let's start with how to read a test.
Game strategy: Teaching point	Reading a test is similar to other reading you do, except you must be sure to read even more carefully than you usually do. When you read a test, you read to answer the questions correctly. Unlike reading your favorite book before you turn out the light at night, you are not reading to relax or fall asleep. You have to stay alert and pay attention to what you are reading, remembering as much as you can. All readers have two voices in their heads: the interacting and the distracting. The interacting voice talks back to the text and the distracting voice takes you away from the text. You want to engage your interacting voice while reading a test. Listen to me read this aloud. I will tell you what I am thinking so you can hear my interacting and my distracting voices. Notice how I pull myself back to the text and how I decide if I need to go back and reread or go on reading. (Teachers, prepare this reading and think-aloud beforehand. Pay attention to your two voices. Don't fake it. Look at the examples in this section to give you ideas for the kinds of thinking aloud you can do with your text. Write your thoughts on sticky notes as you become aware of them and place them in the appropriate spot in the text. Be sure to model distinct differences between these two voices. Read aloud a section of a content area textbook, from a released test selection, a short story, or Bob's Market included here. You can find your state's test by going to this Web site: http://www.aea267.k12.ia.us/cia/math/stateitems.html. Use one passage in three chunks to do this reading: First you read aloud to model; then students read in pairs; finally students finish reading individually.)

Skill practice: Try it in partnerships	Students, continue reading the next section of the selection with your partner. Stop occasionally and share your interacting thoughts and, if you were distracted, share how you got back to thinking about the text.
Own it: Independent practice	Students, as you continue to read the final section of this passage, pay attention to your interacting and distracting voices. What did you miss while being distracted? Did you go back and reread or read on? Why?
Huddle: Assess and reflect	(Have students share their experiences with the class. Be sure to include talk about how they noticed they were distracted and what they did when they went back to their reading.)
Review game strategy: Link	Remember it is important to use your interacting voice while reading a test. Keep your distracting voice quiet.
Closing the session	(In their game plan books, have students record notes about this strategy in their own words. If you are charting the strategies, create a chart titled "Test-Reading Game Strategies" and record *"Keep your interacting voice loud and clear"* as the first strategy.)

─── **Life Skills Connection** ───

Readers read in different ways depending on their purpose. Knowing your purpose for reading determines how you read. Throughout your life, you will set a purpose for your reading and read in different ways. For example, when you read a magazine for pleasure, you may choose to skip around through the magazine, only reading the articles that are of interest to you, and it may not be important if you become distracted. However, when you read a chapter in a science book that you know you will be tested on, you will read slowly, stay engaged with the text, and take notes, so that you can recall the information when needed.

What other real-life connections can you suggest to help your students see the relevance of this game strategy?

• • •

GAME STRATEGY: REREADING

Rereading is one the hallmarks of a strategic reader. It can be challenging to convince struggling readers that rereading is not a weakness, but a strength. As the expert reader in your classroom, modeling how you reread can provide powerful lessons. Think of your own reading. You reread when you are confused. You may even reread something four or five times to be sure you understand it, especially if it is something you do not read all of the time, such as directions or legal documents.

Kelly Gallagher (2004) writes about his students' "I read it—I'm done" attitude in his book, *Deeper Reading*. They expect to read something once and understand it. Gallagher knows he must read text many, many times to fully understand it, especially if the text is complex, and that he must model this for his students if he expects them to do the same.

Usually, during the first read, readers read to see how the whole text fits together. When they read a narrative, they predict how the characters will solve the problem and what will happen next; they then read on to see if they are right.

The second read is different. Readers know all of the above. They now read for details and for what they missed. They experience a cognitive shift away from grasping the gist of the whole text to the details. They know how the characters solved their problems; they can rest on this knowledge and reread for the details they missed the first time through.

> **TIME-OUT**
>
> **What information comes to your attention when you reread?**
>
> Choose a piece of text to read for the first time. Watch your thinking. What are you looking for, wondering about? Next reread the same text. Pay attention to your thinking this time. Compare your thinking with a partner.
>
> 1. What do you notice during the reread?
>
> 2. What information comes to your attention that did not on the first read?

In Figure 2.3, notice how readers might approach this article for a second read. Since they already know what to expect, they are prepared to notice and mark or highlight the important details. As a result, they can put the small details in relationship to each other by creating a Venn diagram.

Figure 2.3   Rereading Sample

Text	Sample Reader Observations on a Second Read
	This time I will underline how they are the same and circle how they are different as I reread this.
Butterflies are colorful, flying insects from the Lepidoptera order. Because they are insects, they have three body	

Text	Sample Reader Observations on a Second Read
parts. The three body parts are called <u>the head, thorax, and abdomen</u>. They also have <u>six jointed legs, two knobbed antennae, compound eyes, and an exoskeleton.</u> Butterflies' four wings are unusual, because they are scaly. Their bodies are covered in little hairs. To eat, butterflies use their long,	I remember when I read it the first time, it said the moth had the same body parts as the butterfly, so I'll underline the names of all the body parts.
straw-like tongues, called <u>a proboscis.</u> They <u>sip nectar from flowers.</u> They keep their proboscis coiled up when they are not eating and uncoil it to drink. Because butterflies and moths are so	The moth has a proboscis too and eats like a butterfly. I can picture the proboscis is like our garden hose when we put it away all curled up.
similar, people confuse these two insects. While they are similar, they are not the same. Moths are also from the <u>Lepidoptera order</u> and they have the	This next part is confusing because it talks about how they are alike and different all together. Both insects are from the same order, so I underline it.
<u>same body parts as a butterfly,</u> except their antennae are not knobbed. Both butterflies and moths have <u>four wings.</u> On the other hand, the moth's body is hairier than the butterfly's body.	Here's where it says they have the same body parts that I underlined above, except I have to circle the information about the antennae because they are different. Both have four wings, so I will underline that, but the moth's body is hairier, so I'll circle it.
Moths <u>use a proboscis to eat just like the butterfly does.</u> They both sip nectar from flowers.	They are alike here, so I will underline it.
There are two big differences between these two insects. One difference is butterflies fly in the daytime and moths fly at nighttime. Butterflies hold their wings closed above their bodies when they are standing still. In contrast, moths hold their open wings out to their sides when not flying.	The rest is about how they are different, so I will circle the details. I can make a Venn diagram with this information.

Teachers, if your test is timed, you may not emphasize deep rereading as a second read, since rereading the entire passage slowly would take up too much time. If time is an issue, teach students to skim for the second read.

Game Plan Practice Session

Rereading

Equipment	• Released test passages or content area textbook • Game plan books • Chart paper and markers or transparency of the strategies
Connection	Team, get your game plan books, it's time for today's game strategy. You are about to learn another fail-proof reading strategy. You learned how to stay focused on your reading, even if it is the most boring selection you ever read. Today we are continuing our study of how to beat the test by learning a new strategy to use while reading.
Game strategy: Teaching point	Rereading is a valuable reading strategy. Readers reread for two reasons: to clear up confusion and to pay attention to missed details. Students, many of you may think that rereading is a weakness and that only poor readers reread. This is not true. As a good reader myself, and someone who hangs around a lot of good readers, I can assure you that effective readers reread all of the time. They are aware of what is confusing as they read. They decide whether to reread or not, depending on their purpose for reading. Of course on a test, you should reread frequently to ensure your comprehension. Rereading also helps you notice details you may have missed on your first read. Listen as I reread this to you. Watch me stop and check my understanding. If I don't get it, watch what I do. See how I decide how far back to reread. Also, listen to what I noticed on the second read that I may have missed the first time I read this. Think of rereading like practicing for any sport. You practice plays over and over to perfect them, usually with the coach telling you what you did well and what to change. You will act as your own coach as you read, noticing when you are confused so you know when to reread or how to reread to see what you missed the first time through. (Teachers, be sure to reread a text from an earlier lesson for this next section. Prepare this lesson ahead of time, using sticky notes to record what confused you and what you noticed on your second read. Don't fake it. If this is a new concept for your students, break this lesson into two: one emphasizing rereading to clear up confusion and another emphasizing rereading to fill in details that slipped by on a first read.)
Skill practice: Try it in partnerships	Partners, continue rereading the next part of this selection. Stop occasionally and tell your partner what details you notice today. Rereading not only anchors the text in your head, it also allows you to notice details you may have missed on your first reading.

Own it: Independent practice	Now, students, you will continue rereading the final section on your own. Watch to see when you reread. Were you confused? Were you distracted? Did rereading help?
Huddle: Assess and reflect	(Have students share their experiences with the class. Talk about rereading to clear up confusion and rereading to notice details.)
Review game strategy: Link	Remember, as you read the test you may have to reread to be sure you understand what you have read and to notice important details.
Closing the session	(In their game plan books, have students record notes about this strategy in their own words. If you are charting the strategies, add *"Reread to notice important details and clear up confusion"* to the "Test-Reading Game Strategies" chart.)

Life Skills Connection

Readers reread when they are confused, distracted, or reading complex text. When reading text you are not accustomed to reading, such as the directions for a camera, you may find yourself reverting to many early reader tactics: slowing down; saying the words aloud; and rereading over and over again.

What other real-life connections can you suggest to help your students see the relevance of this game strategy?

• • •

GAME STRATEGY: EXPOSITORY TEXT STRUCTURES

Readers can see relationships between small pieces of information in expository text if they understand how the text is organized. Understanding how a text is organized assists them as they comprehend what they are reading (Montelongo & Hernandez, 2007). The five most common expository structures are description, sequential, compare and contrast, problem-solution, and cause and effect. Knowing these structures will help students as they read English language arts, science, mathematics, and social studies tests.

The following chart in Figure 2.4 includes definitions for the expository text structures and sample word cues for each. If readers understand these structures, they know to expect certain information. For example, if they read words such as *like* and *both*, they know it is comparative text and they will learn how certain ideas are alike. When reading text that contrasts, readers encounter words such as *on the other hand*, *but*, and *in this case*. These words position the ideas by how they differ from each other.

When readers understand text structure, they anticipate and can fit small pieces of information together into a larger concept. The word cues situate the ideas in relationship to each other. They show how they are connected. Readers understand how the sections fit together to build the entire piece. If readers don't catch or understand these word cues, they may misunderstand the entire section. Struggling readers often misread these small cue words, and this explains why they do not correctly comprehend expository text.

Figure 2.4   Expository Text Structures

Text Structure	Definition	Word Cues
Description	Information gives visual details	Specific words that tell what something is like; adjectives and similes may be used
Sequential	Information presented in chronological order from beginning to end	First, second, third, next, then, last, later, after, finally, at last
Compare and contrast	Information shows how two or more items are alike and different	Compare: just like, as well as, both, alike, also, same, similar, compare Contrast: different, differences, not alike, contrast, except, but, yet, on the other hand, however, while
Problem-solution	Information poses a problem and possible solution	Because, problem, solution, question, so that
Cause and effect	Information explains why something happened	Because, the reason for, thus, since, consequently, if . . . then, as a result, the cause(s) is/are

Rarely does a piece of text of any length follow only one structure, which can make recognizing text structure more challenging. For example, while looking at a social studies textbook, the first paragraph of a section *describes* the United States House of Representatives. The next paragraph begins *describing* the United States Senate, but quickly switches to *contrasting* it with the House of Representatives. Students must be alert to these changes in text structures to facilitate their understanding in the everyday learning they do in their classrooms. They will also need to use this skill while reading a test.

Examine the text in Figure 2.5. It is composed of two kinds of expository text: descriptive and compare and contrast. Watch for the shifts between each type of text. The right side of the chart offers some suggested observations you might make.

Figure 2.5   Sample Reader Observations of Expository Text Structures

Text	Sample Reader Observations of Expository Text Structures
Interesting Insects	
	From the title, I am assuming this is expository text. I know it will help me to understand the text better if I know the text structure. I am going to pay attention to how it is organized.
Butterflies are colorful, flying insects from the Lepidoptera order. Because they are insects, they have three body	
parts. The three body parts are called the head, thorax, and abdomen. They also have six jointed legs, two knobbed antennae, compound eyes, and an exoskeleton.	This seems to be descriptive writing. The words are making a picture in my head of what a butterfly looks like.
Butterflies' four wings are unusual, because they are scaly. Their bodies are covered in little hairs.	This is descriptive writing too.
To eat, butterflies use their long, straw-like tongue, called a proboscis. They sip nectar from flowers. They keep their proboscis coiled up when they are not eating and uncoil it to drink.	I still think this is descriptive writing, because this is almost like a simile. It said the tongue is like a straw. I get that.
Because butterflies and moths are so similar, people confuse these two insects. While they are similar, they are not the same. Moths are also from the Lepidoptera order and they have the same	This part seems to change. It's not only talking about butterflies now. It is also talking about moths. The words "also" and "same" are telling how they are alike, so this is comparative text.
body parts as butterfly, except their	But the word "except" now tells me how they are different, so it is contrast writing.

(Continued)

Figure 2.5 (Continued)

Text	Sample Reader Observations of Expository Text Structures
antennae are not knobbed. Both butterflies and moths have four wings. On the other hand, the moth's body is hairier than the butterfly's body. Moths use a proboscis to eat just like the butterfly does. They both sip nectar from flowers. There are two big differences between these two insects. One difference is butterflies fly in the daytime and moths fly at nighttime. Butterflies hold their wings closed above their bodies when they are standing still. In contrast, moths hold their open wings out to their sides when not flying.	The word "both" tells me they are alike again. Then this sentence says "on the other hand," and I know they are different again. It seems like some of the sentences are comparing and some are contrasting moths and butterflies. I have to read carefully so I understand how these two insects are alike and different.

If this is a new concept for your students, you may want to do this lesson with passages that are written specifically with these structures in mind such as the book by Boynton and Blevins (2003), *Teaching Students to Read Nonfiction*. Once your students are familiar with the language shifts in each structure, do this lesson using your content area textbooks.

Game Plan Practice Session

Expository Text Structures

Equipment	• Released test passages or content area textbook on an overhead • Expository Text Structures on a transparency • Optional "Interesting Insects" transparency • Game plan books • Chart paper and markers or transparency of the strategies
Connection	Team, get your game plan books, it's time for today's game strategy. Today you will learn to unlock the mysteries of expository text. You will read expository text and examine the text structure. This will help you read more effectively in school, on tests, and in life!

Game strategy: Teaching point	An additional way to use your interacting voice is to pay close attention to how expository text is structured. There are five basic expository text structures: description, cause and effect, compare and contrast, problem-solution, and sequential. When we understand how the text is organized, we better understand the ideas presented. We can see the relationships between the ideas. Look at this chart of the text structures. (Show Figure 2.4, Expository Text Structures). These words cues are important in understanding how the text is organized.
	Now look at this selection. I will read this page to you and think aloud as I identify the text structure of the writing, explaining how I knew it was a certain kind of text. (See Figure 2.5, Sample Reader Observations of Expository Text Structures, for a model of a think-aloud.)
	(Teachers, find a page or section that demonstrates some of these text structures from a content area textbook or a released test selection. You can also use the passage "Interesting Insects." Read the passage aloud and mark the words that cued you to know what kind of text this is. Explain how the words show the relationship between the ideas.)
Skill practice: Try it in partnerships	Students, read another section of the text with your partner. Together identify the kind of expository text structure that is used and explain the word cues that led you to your decisions.
Own it: Independent practice	Students, as you continue reading on your own, watch for shifts in text structure. Remember, the word cues will help you to know when the text structure changes. Circle them as you read.
Huddle: Assess and reflect	(Have students share what kinds of text structures they found and how they identified them. Have them explain how the word clues showed the relationship between concepts.)
Review game strategy: Link	Remember, when reading expository text, you will understand it more completely if you know how it is organized.
Closing the session	(In their game plan books, have students record notes about this strategy in their own words.
	If you are charting the strategies, add *"Notice the text structure of expository text by watching the word cues; they will help you understand the text and know what is important"* to the "Test-Reading Game Strategies" chart.)

GAME STRATEGY: READING GRAPHICS

Information needed for answering test questions is not always located in written passages. Test takers also need to look at graphics, such as charts, graphs, and maps to get information for answering questions. Graphics visually show relationships between concepts and data. They assist readers in understanding the written text by exemplifying and extending what is written. Strategic readers know how to read and gather information from a variety of graphics.

Please note that preparing for a test is not the time to teach each graphic listed in Figure 2.6; you will teach students how to read and infer information from graphics over the course of a school year. For this strategy lesson, look at your state test and focus on the type of graphics that are featured. Math, science, and social studies tests appear to include a wide range and frequent use of graphics.

Figure 2.6 Types of Graphics

Bar Graphs	Maps
Charts	Paintings
Diagrams	Photographs
Drawings	Pie Graphs
Illustrations	Tables
Line Graphs	Timelines

Writers include graphics because they are an efficient way to portray large amounts of information in a small amount of space. Readers study graphics to extract literal (in the text) and inferential (in your head) information. The specific data in a graphic are the literal information, but the relationships between the information must be inferred.

Test questions that refer to a graphic focus the reader's attention. When asking for direct information, the reader simply lifts it off the graphic and answers the question. However, when the question asks for an interpretation of data, the reader infers the relationships between what is presented.

Examine the line graph in Figure 2.7. If a question asks, "At what time was it the hottest on July 4th?" test takers would look at the graph to find the peak temperature and corresponding time of day and find the matching answer on the test. This is a literal question. If the question asks "What is the difference in temperature from the hottest and coolest times on July 4th?" test takers must determine a mathematical process to perform to obtain the relationship between the two temperatures and determine the answer. In this case, they will subtract the temperature at 5:00 a.m. from the temperature at 5:00 p.m. After calculating this number, they will find the answer on the test that matches. This is an inferential question.

TIME-OUT

How do I approach various graphics in expository text?

Review your state science, social studies, and math tests. What graphics are included? Choose one to examine. Be metacognitive as you examine the graphic. Compare your thinking with a partner's.

1. As you examined the graphic, what did you look at first?

2. Did you read the title? The labels? The data given?

3. What information is explicitly given?

4. What can you infer from the data presented?

Figure 2.7   Line Graph

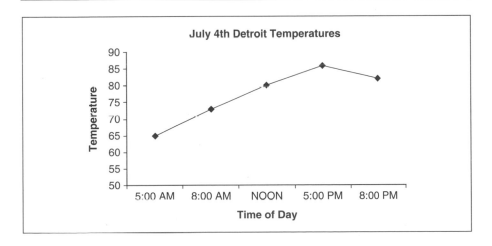

Game Plan Practice Session

Reading Graphics

Equipment	• Released test items using graphics • One released test item with a graphic on an overhead • "Types of Graphics" on an overhead • "July 4th Detroit Temperatures" graphic on an overhead • Game plan books • Chart paper and markers or transparency of the strategies
Connection	Team, get your game plan books, it's time for today's game strategy. Every day you learn another test-taking strategy, the smarter you get! Today you'll learn a totally different kind of reading. Some questions ask a reader to find information in a graphic. You will learn to read graphics so you can answer those questions correctly.
Game strategy: Teaching point	Writers use graphics to include a lot of information in a small amount of space. (Teachers, using the line graph example above, model for students how you approach this graphic.) When you examine a graph, first look at the title, then look at axis labels, and then the specific times named and the temperatures given. Now that you have an overview of the graph, you ask yourself, "What is this graphic showing me about this information? I see the temperature rose steadily during the day until 5:00 p.m. and then it began to cool down. Now I will read the question to see what it wants me to know about this graph." (Teachers, read the first question aloud and think aloud explaining how you determined the answer. Then read the second question and think aloud demonstrating how you arrived at that answer. Be sure to show the difference between how you got your answers for each question. You may choose to use the questions above or an appropriate item from your released state test. If you choose to use a test item, demonstrate the following steps as you study a graph. • Read the title. • Read the labels and the key. • Look at the specific information in the graph. • Ask yourself "What is the graph showing me about this information? How is it related?")
Skill practice: Try it in partnerships	Students, look at this test item that includes a graphic with your partner. Work together to decide on the correct answer. You will share your thinking with the class.

Own it: Independent practice	Students, now you will try another question on your own. Remember some questions ask for specific information from the graphic, but most questions require you to infer the relationships between information.
Huddle: Assess and reflect	(Have students share how they arrived at the answer to the question.)
Review game strategy: Link	Remember, graphics visually present how information is related. Use the following steps as you find information on a graph: 1. Read the title. 2. Read the labels and key. 3. Look at the specific information in the graph. 4. Ask yourself "What is the graph showing me about this information? How is it related?"
Closing the session	(In their game plan books, have students record notes about this strategy in their own words. If you are charting the strategies, add *"Study graphics carefully to see how the information presented is related"* to the "Test-Reading Game Strategies" chart.)

─────── **Life Skills Connection** ───────

Readers encounter graphics in many forms. Some assembly instructions include few words and many diagrams of how to put each section together. You study the diagrams carefully before gathering the appropriate pieces and beginning to assemble the parts.

What other real-life connections can you suggest to help your students see the relevance of this game strategy?

• • •

GAME STRATEGY: NARRATIVE TEXT STRUCTURES

As in expository text, there is a narrative text structure. Students who understand narrative text structure read stories anticipating the author will provide essential information. They expect to read about the characters, setting, plot (problem and solution), and theme of the story. They read looking for these details. Their sense of story includes these parts; it provides a structure for them. Story structure holds the details together into a narrative.

Figure 2.8 depicts what a reader might think about while watching for the elements of narrative text. These elements focus readers on the structure and help them to hone in on what is important so they can remember these parts.

Figure 2.8 Sample Reader Observations of Narrative Text Structure

Text	Sample Reader Observations of Narrative Text Structures
Bob's Market	
It was a usual Saturday. But sometimes important lessons happen on ordinary days. Betty, Connie, Kim, and I went to Bob's Market for penny candy. Bob always teased me about being short, and I always ignored him. But everyone else laughed.	I see it is a Saturday. That is part of the setting. There are four characters so far. One of them is telling the story. They are in a store buying some kind of candy. This is sounds like a story and not expository text.
After picking our candy, we	
went around the corner into the alley along the back of the market toward the railroad tracks and the woods between our neighborhood and the high school.	The setting has changed. Now they are in an alley. There is not a lot around there because there are woods and railroad tracks.
Connie noticed the sheet of glass. The corner was broken, and it leaned against the trash bins. Betty said, "We should break it."	This looks like it could be the problem.
"Yeah, great idea. Me first," Kim and Connie said together.	
Then they threw a handful of pebbles. Nothing happened. Betty threw two large rocks. Nothing happened. Then I picked up a huge boulder. I stood right next to the glass and threw the rock down. The glass broke with a loud crash.	
Almost immediately, Betty, Connie, and Kim cheered.	
And Bob slammed the screen door at the back of the market. We looked at Bob simultaneously. Connie yelled, "Run!" And everyone ran, including me. At the end of the alley, I stopped. Why had I run away? What was I thinking?	The problem gets worse here, because Bob saw them. They choose to run away. That could make this problem worse too.
We rounded the corner at the end of the block, and Betty kept telling how I found the biggest rock, how I threw the hardest, and the best, how I broke the window. Kim just stared at	
me, and I knew that she would tell Mom when we got home. She always told. I didn't care about any of that. I could only think of Bob.	The problem is getting worse for the narrator, because her sister is going to tell their mom.
"I'm going back. We have to turn	
ourselves in. He knows us," I said.	The narrator suggests a possible solution, but the rest of the characters disagree.
"No way. He doesn't know me," Betty said.	
"Me either."	
"I didn't do anything," said Kim.	
"Well, he knows me, and I broke the window, and I have to go back."	

Text	Sample Reader Observations of Narrative Text Structures
"Well, I'm not."	
"See ya at school."	
"I'm going home and tell Mom," Kim said.	
I walked back to Bob's alone. He was waiting behind the counter. There was no smile on his face. I walked straight up to the counter and	
apologized. He didn't yell. He just handed me a broom.	The narrator solves the problem by going back to apologize.
For the next week I swept floors and	
carried out trash after school. To be honest, I enjoyed it. I knew I was wrong, and it was better to face my mistake and make it right.	If I think of setting, characters, problem, and solution, I can remember and retell this story easily.
It was a good lesson to learn at 10 years old.	Theme: Honesty is the best policy.

Game Plan Practice Session

Narrative Text Structures

Equipment	• Released test passages • Overhead of test passage • Game plan books • Chart paper and markers or transparency of the strategies
Connection	Team, get your game plan books, it's time for today's game strategy. You are coming into the home stretch of reading strategies. Because you read stories, you are familiar with narrative text structure. Today you will learn how to use that structure to remember or find important facts from the selection so you answer questions correctly.
Game strategy: Teaching point	Another way to use your interacting voice when you are taking a reading test is to watch the essential parts of the narrative you find in the text: characters, setting, plot (problem and solution), and theme of the story. It's just like what we study when we read stories in class, except the passages will be in the test, not in a book.

(Continued)

(Continued)

Game strategy: Teaching point	I will begin to read this story aloud to you. As I do, listen as I share with you what I am thinking when I notice the essential elements of the narrative and how noticing this information holds the story together. Paying attention to these details, anchors them in my memory. I will make notes in the margins as I read from this overhead. I will mark a
	
	    C when I encounter information about the characters,
	
	    S when I encounter information about the setting,
	
	    P when I encounter information about the problem,
	
	    SL when I encounter information about the solution.
	
	I will state the theme for this story as I think aloud.
	
	(Teachers, read the text ahead of time. Make notes of the essential elements. It's best to use a released passage from your state's test. As you read aloud to your students, stop and comment when you notice the elements. Each time, look up from the text and use a conversational voice so the students can distinguish between your reading voice and your think-aloud, conversational voice.)

Skill practice: Try it in partnerships	Partners, continue reading this selection. Make notes in the margin as you read. Mark a
	
	    C when you encounter information about the characters,
	
	    S when you encounter information about the setting,
	
	    P when you encounter information about the problem,
	
	    SL when you encounter information about the solution.
	
	Check to see if the two of you marked the same information. Discuss what you think the theme of the story is.

Own it: Independent practice	Now, students, continue reading or read the new passage on your own. Continue to make marginal notes of essential story elements. See if making notes of this information helps you remember it or find it each time you read.
Huddle: Assess and reflect	(Have students share their experiences and marginal notes with the class. Be sure to include how knowing these parts helps them to anticipate what is revealed in the story.)
Review game strategy: Link	Remember as you read narrative passages on a reading test, make notes of the essential story information. The test questions will relate to this essential information. (Teachers, if students are allowed to write in their test booklets, strongly urge them to make marginal notes as above or highlight this information.)

Closing the session	(In their game plan books, have students record notes about this strategy in their own words.
	If you are charting the strategies, add *"When reading narrative text, pay attention to the characters, setting, plot (problem and solution), and theme of the story"* to the "Test-Reading Game Strategies" chart.)

Life Skills Connection

Readers rely on narrative authors to give them essential information about the setting, characters, and plot. They anticipate this information and read with this frame in mind. When authors fail to make this information clear, you may get confused and not like the book.

What other real-life connections can you suggest to help your students see the relevance of this game strategy?

• • •

GAME STRATEGY: WATCHING THE CHARACTERS

The characters in a story are one piece of essential information. They are the actors who guide us through the story as we read (Roser, Martinez, Fuhrken, & McDonald, 2007). Their motivations drive the story; they are the reason the story is happening. Sometimes characters' motivations are in conflict with other characters, and other times they work toward a common goal. If characters and their wants drive stories, students must understand the importance of watching the characters carefully.

While reading a test, readers also pay attention to the characters; they watch them as they move through the story. On a test, readers do this, not only because it is what they do, but because they know that questions will ask about the characters. If there is an extended or constructed response question, the answer will probably include details about the characters as substantiation. The characters' actions and words may relate to the theme of the selection, and test takers will use them as evidence.

Teach students to love and watch characters as they read during the school year. Then at test-taking time, teach them to use this strategy as a tool to successfully answer questions on a test by observing characters closely.

In Figure 2.9, the reader watches the main character closely. The reader questions certain behaviors and notices when the main character changes during the story.

Figure 2.9 Sample Interacting Voice—Character Observations

Text	Sample Reader Observations of Characters
Bob's Market	
It was a usual Saturday. But sometimes important lessons happen on ordinary days. Betty, Connie, Kim, and I went to Bob's Market for penny candy. Bob always teased me about being short, and I always ignored him. But everyone else laughed.	There are four characters in this story. One of them is telling the story. I wonder how the fact the narrator is being teased will play out in the story.
After picking our candy, we	
went around the corner into the alley along the back of the market toward the railroad tracks and the woods between our neighborhood and the high school.	
Connie noticed the sheet of glass. The corner was broken, and it leaned against the trash bins. Betty said, "We should break it."	Betty is the leader here, but Kim and Connie want to be first.
"Yeah, great idea. Me first," Kim and Connie said together.	
Then they threw a handful of pebbles. Nothing happened. Betty threw two large rocks. Nothing happened. Then I picked up a huge boulder. I stood right next to the glass and threw the rock down. The glass broke with a loud crash.	Just throwing pebbles seems like a half-hearted attempt to break the glass. I don't think they really want to break it. The narrator wants to break it. He or she uses something big enough to do so on the first try. I think this character is trying to prove something here. Maybe being teased about being short has an influence on this behavior. The narrator is trying to prove him or herself.
Almost immediately, Betty, Connie, and Kim cheered.	
And Bob slammed the screen door at the back of the market. We looked at Bob simultaneously. Connie yelled, "Run!" And everyone ran, including me. At the end of the alley, I stopped. Why had I run away? What was I thinking?	
We rounded the corner at the end of the block, and Betty kept telling how I found the biggest rock, how I threw the hardest and the best, how I broke the window. Kim just stared a	The narrator seems to have a change of heart. Once Bob saw them, the narrator realized it was not just breaking a piece of glass that was in the alley; it was an act against someone they knew and it was wrong.

Text	Sample Reader Observations of Characters
me, and I knew that she would tell Mom when we got home. She always told. I didn't care about any of that. I could only think of Bob.	
"I'm going back. We have to turn	
ourselves in. He knows us," I said.	
"No way. He doesn't know me," Betty said.	
"Me either."	
"I didn't do anything," said Kim.	
"Well, he knows me, and I broke the window, and I have to go back."	
"Well, I'm not."	
"See ya at school."	
"I'm going home and tell Mom," Kim said.	
I walked back to Bob's alone. He was waiting behind the counter. There was no smile on his face. I walked straight up to the counter an	The narrator follows through on his or her instincts of what is right and wrong.
apologized. He didn't yell. He just handed me a broom.	
For the next week I swept floors and carried out trash after school. To be honest, I enjoyed it. I knew I was wrong, and it was better to face my mistake and make it right.	While the other characters did not change during this story, the narrator did.
It was a good lesson to learn at 10 years old.	The narrator learned a lesson about honesty and facing a mistake.

Game Plan Practice Session

Watching the Characters

Equipment	• Released test passages • Game plan books • Chart paper and markers or transparency of the strategies
Connection	Team, get your game plan books, it's time for today's game strategy. First, let's look at all of the strategies you have learned so far: • Keep your interactive voice loud and clear. • Reread to notice important details and clear up confusion. • Notice the text structure of expository text by watching the word cues; they will help you understand the text and know what is important. • Study graphics carefully to see how the information presented is related. • When reading narrative text, pay attention to the characters, setting, plot (problem and solution), and theme of the story. Today you will learn the last game strategy for reading on a test.
Game strategy: Teaching point	While reading on a test, you can use your interacting voice to watch the characters carefully. You will watch how they change and what they want. Today I will show you what I do as I read. (Teachers, read the text ahead of time, making notes of the main characters' motivations, actions, and changes.) Readers watch the characters as they read. They also know the story is about what the characters want, what they do, and how they change. The characters are the actors in the story and guide you through the story. As I read this aloud to you, I will stop and share my interacting voice with you. I will tell you what I notice about the characters. (Teachers, be sure to choose text that has strong character development for this lesson. It's best to use a released passage from your state's test. Stop reading partway through.)
Skill practice: Try it in partnerships	Partners, continue reading this selection. Stop occasionally and share what you notice about the characters. Note the characters' actions and what they want.
Own it: Independent practice	Now, students, you will continue reading on your own. Think of the characters as actors in a play who guide you through the story. Pay especially close attention to the main characters. Watch to see if they change.

Huddle: Assess and reflect	(Have students share their experiences with the class. Do they all agree on what kind of person the main character is? Do they agree on what the main character wants? Have the characters changed?)
Review game strategy: Link	Remember as you read, watch the characters carefully. Questions will be asked about them and you may use their actions, motivations, or words to answer them.
Closing the session	(In their game plan books, have students record notes about this strategy in their own words. If you are charting the strategies, add: "Pay close attention to • what the characters want • what the characters do • whether the characters change" to the "Test-Reading Game Strategies" chart.) Students, be sure to treat your game plan book with care. It holds valuable information. You do not want to lose it.

Life Skills Connection

Readers know how stories go. They know the characters drive the plot. When reading a novel, they connect with the characters and watch them as the story unfolds. It's like when you go to see a movie, you expect it to have characters that you connect to. If the characters are not appealing, you probably won't like the movie.

What other real-life connections can you suggest to help your students see the relevance of this game strategy?

• • •

Test-Reading Game Strategies

- Keep your interactive voice loud and clear.
- Reread to notice important details and clear up confusion.
- Notice the text structure of expository text by watching the word cues; they will help you understand the text and know what is important.
- Study graphics carefully to see how the information presented is related.
- When reading narrative text, pay attention to the characters, setting, plot (problem and solution), and theme of the story.
- Pay close attention to

1. what the characters want
2. what the characters do
3. whether the characters change

ASSESSMENT

During this course of study, you offered your students many scaffolded opportunities to learn and put into practice the test-reading strategies through modeling and paired and individual work. Using the checklist in Figure 2.10, students remind themselves to use the strategies and then assess how effectively they used them. At this point, you are moving them toward independent use.

Using Figure 2.10 as a guide, create a Test-Reading Strategies Checklist for each student. While reading a released test selection, have students complete the checklist by placing a check mark in the first column next to each strategy used. If they are able to do so, instruct students to make comments on when they were aware of using a strategy.

Once complete, instruct them to discuss with a partner if they used a strategy, when, and why. They will not use every strategy for every reading; two strategies are specific to narrative and two are intended for expository reading. This type of reflection encourages students to become metacognitive while reading, reflecting on intentional strategy use.

Circulate the room, listening to the comments students make. What are they doing well? What do you need to reinforce or reteach?

FINAL THOUGHTS

You cannot teach reading strategies only as preparation for a high-stakes test. Then it is too late. Regularly embed the teaching of reading strategies into your teaching in all content areas. Then as you prepare students for a test, remind them of the reading strategies you taught over the course of a school year. You teach them what you know about reading: the voices in your head, narrative, expository text structures, graphics, and why you reread. At test prep time, you review and remind them of these strategies and how to transfer them to a test-taking situation.

Figure 2.10   Test-Reading Strategies Checklist

I Remembered to	Comments (Sample Student Comments)
Keep my interacting voice loud and clear.	I got distracted when I heard other kids talking, but I reminded myself to go back to my interacting voice quickly.
Reread to notice important details and clear up confusion.	I wasn't sure what they meant in this section so I reread the last two paragraphs and it made sense.
Notice the text structure of expository text by watching the word cues.	I read the words first, next, and last and knew it was written in sequential order and that the order is important.
Study graphics to decide how the information is related.	I looked at the bar graph and decided how the information was connected.
Watch for the characters, setting, plot, and theme of the story.	I knew this was a story because there were characters. I then knew there would be a problem and a solution.
Pay close attention to what the characters want, what they do, and if they change.	The character in my story was in a plane crash and was alone. I knew the story would be about if he survived or not.

Question-Answering Strategies

3

Although we still went over the questions and talked about the answers, our emphasis now was on the strategies children had used or might have used to reach these answers.

—Calkins, Montgomery, Falk, and Santman (1998, p. 106)

GAME STRATEGY FOR STUDENTS

Understand That . . .

- Test writers use specific techniques to develop test questions and answer choices, and when test takers understand these techniques, they can take tests more effectively.
- Effective test takers have a tool kit of strategies they use to read and answer test questions.

Know

- How to eliminate answers on standardized tests

Able to Do

- Answer standardized test questions correctly

CHEAT CODES

Teaching students the specific techniques used to develop test questions and answer choices helps them to take tests more effectively. As effective test takers, they have a tool kit of strategies they use to read and answer test questions. These strategies empower students to have a "can do" attitude when it comes to taking tests.

Video game players see themselves as "gamers." They do not rely only on their gaming skills; they work to maximize their play by visiting online sites to learn cheat codes from other "gamers." These cheat codes help players maximize their video play by manipulating the game's program and enhancing aspects of the game. They might be as simple as adding ammunition to a weapon or as complex as making a character invincible. Cheat codes give players an inside edge on playing a game successfully. A video game player gains these cheat codes by learning to read and think in specific ways (Gee, 2003, pp. 100–103). In *What Video Games Have to Teach Us About Learning and Literacy*, researcher James Paul Gee suggests membership combined with knowledge and literacy habits develop a skilled player. The social nature of the network enables players to become far more successful than one might expect and better than an individual's original self-assessment. In effect, the distribution of knowledge (in this case, video game cheat codes) and the social encounters in a network of players make an individual more successful (Gee, 2003, pp. 184–189).

Test-reading strategies give students a similar edge when preparing for a standardized test in a conversational classroom that work like a video game online network or a team. The payoff for team members occurs when they take a standardized test. Smart test takers understand how questions and answers function. They have the inside scoop on how tests operate so they can maximize their chances of success. With this inside information, students make the best decisions while answering questions. As you teach the strategies in this section, be sure to strengthen the connection between these strategies and gaming cheat codes by calling the question-answering strategies game strategies.

As you read the examples in this chapter, be metacognitive—think about your own thinking. Note how you think to eliminate incorrect answers. Think aloud to teach the strategies so that students own and transfer them. As the expert test taker, you are coaching your students on how to think while they independently take the test.

GAME STRATEGY: UNDERSTANDING QUESTIONS THAT HAVE "ALMOST RIGHT" ANSWERS

To be thoughtful test takers, students need to know how the answers are created for standardized tests. When four answer choices are given, many times two choices can be eliminated immediately. These two answer choices are obviously incorrect. Of the two choices left, one answer choice is the best or right answer, but the other answer choice may be the "almost right" answer. This answer choice distracts students from the right answer, especially if it is the first answer choice.

Test makers include "almost right" answers, or distracters, not to trick children, but to discern those who really know the information from those who do not. On a math test, test makers move the decimal one way or the other or flip a fraction to create an "almost right" answer. They can be found on all types of standardized tests.

Some test reports show how many students chose each answer choice for the questions. Many times the choices cluster around two, the right answer and the "almost right" answer. Students must be prepared to reread to verify answers.

Examples

1. *Fourth-Grade Example From 2002 Georgia Criterion-Referenced Competency Test Released Items*
   Which word has a prefix that means *to do again?*

   A. register
   B. determine
   C. rediscover
   D. defrost

Explanation. In this question, *register* is the "almost right" answer choice because it begins with *re*. As answer choice A, it serves as a strong distracter. Even if students know the prefix *re* means to do again, they still have to determine that *re* in register is not a prefix. The correct answer is C.

2. *Fourth-Grade Example From 2007 Ohio Achievement Test Released Items*
   Where did John usually plant trees?

   A. in the middle of thick woods
   B. on the bare tops of mountains and hills
   C. in the clearings near rivers and streams
   D. at inns and way stations

Explanation. In this question, answer C is the correct answer choice. Answer D is the "almost right" answer choice. In the selection, Johnny Appleseed left saplings at inns and way stations in exchange for food, clothes, and money. He did not plant trees there.

The following quote from the selection "The Apple-Seed Man" by Paula Appling shows the difference between the two answer choices.

> John planted trees wherever he went, usually in clearings near rivers or streams . . .
>
> Sometimes he let the trees grow right where he had planted them. But usually he'd return after two years and take the saplings, pack them carefully, and leave them at a way station, with a family, or at an inn. . . .

Answer choices A and B are not mentioned in the text and can easily be eliminated.

Game Plan Practice Session

Understanding Questions That Have "Almost Right" Answers

Equipment	• Released test passages on overheads • Sample questions on overheads • Game plan books • Chart paper and markers or transparency of the strategies
Connection	Team, get your game plan books, it's time for today's game strategy. Imagine coming into test day knowing that no matter what question they throw at you, you are ready! That is how you'll feel after you learn the next round of game strategies. In this course of study, you will learn question-answering strategies. In learning to take tests, one of the first things you are going to study is the specific techniques test writers use to develop test questions and answer choices. You will study them because when test takers understand these techniques they can take tests more effectively. In fact, test takers are not the only people who use specific techniques to learn to be better at what they do. Video gamers learn to use cheat codes to enhance their performance while playing video games. They go to online sites to learn how to maximize their play. Learning about tests and how they operate is similar to learning about cheat codes for video games, but we use game strategies that help you to be successful test takers.

Game strategy: Teaching point	Here's your first game strategy. Two answers for one question can appear correct. It is important to distinguish the "almost right" answer from the correct answer choice. On a math test, the decimal might be moved to the right or left and a fraction may be flipped.
	Coaches and team members watch videos of other teams' plays to determine their weaknesses. As test takers, you will know to look for weak spots (wrong answers), to eliminate them and choose between the right answer choice and the "almost right" answer choice.
	(Teachers, it's best to use examples from released items from your state test or a content area test. Find an example that includes an "almost right" answer choice or use one of the samples included here. Show students the question. Point out the two answer choices you are deciding between. Demonstrate how you skim the passage to locate where to look to validate your final choice.)
Skill practice: Try it in partnerships	(After reading a short selection, prepare a question for your students. Give the students the right answer. In pairs, have them write an "almost right" answer for the question and two other wrong answer choices.)
Own it: Independent practice	(Independently, have students study questions with "almost right" answers and explain why they would rule out that answer choice. It's best to use examples from released items from your state test or a content area test. If your students are capable, have them write their own question and answer choices, including an "almost right" answer. This might be hard for some students, especially third graders.)
Huddle: Assess and reflect	(Have students share their questions and answer choices and discuss how they eliminated the "almost right" answer choice.)
Review game strategy: Link	Remember some questions have "almost right" answer choices. It is important to read each answer choice, paying close attention to the details in the answers to decide which one is the right answer.
Closing the session	(In their game plan books, have students record notes about this strategy in their own words.
	If you are charting the strategies, create a chart titled "Question-Answering Game Strategies" and record "*Understanding questions that have 'almost right' answers*" as the first strategy.)

—————————————— **Life Skills Connection** ——————————————

In economics, *opportunity cost* is what you give up when you make a choice. When you choose, you lose the opportunity the other choice offered. Studying the options carefully enhances your chances of making the better choice.

    What other real-life connections can you suggest to help your students see the relevance of this game strategy?

—————————————————— • • • ——————————————

GAME STRATEGY: UNDERSTANDING QUESTIONS THAT USE FACTS FROM THE TEXT AS WRONG ANSWER CHOICES

Test makers use facts from the text as wrong answer choices. Students who do not read carefully may have difficulty choosing from these answers because all of them seem correct. Students must read carefully and make sure their answer choice answers the question asked. While not all questions include answers that are facts from the text, they do exist and can prove to be difficult for students.

Examples

1. *Third-Grade Example From the Fall 2005 Michigan Education Assessment Program (MEAP) Released Items*
   According to Eric, how do lizards talk to each other?

   A. They change colors.
   B. They move their tongues in and out.
   C. They stick out their red throats.

Explanation. Eric watched the lizards do all of these things, but he thought they were talking to each other when they stuck out their red throats. This quote from the selection "Eric's Lizard" by Dave Griswold substantiates answer choice C as the correct answer.

> During the day they sat in the sun. Sometimes they stuck out the red skin on their throats and nodded their heads up and down like little flags. "Are you saying something to each other?" Eric asked.

2. *Seventh-Grade Example From 2003–06 California Standards Test (CST) Released Items*

Houdini decided to become a magician after

A. He read a book about a famous magician.
B. He learned to pick a lock.
C. He started entertaining at local parties.
D. He learned to do card tricks.

Explanation. Houdini did all of these things, but only after he read a book about a famous magician did he decide to become one himself. The following quote from the selection "The Magic of Harry" makes it very clear this is when Harry decided to become a magician.

> When Ehrich was 16, he came across a book that would literally change his life: the biography of France's greatest magician, Jean Eugene Robert-Houdin. It showed Ehrich that his hobby of magic and tricks could also be a career. Immediately, he changed his name to Harry Houdini. He and Theo headed out to make a living as magicians.

All of the answer choices in the questions above may appear correct to the test taker since they all actually happened in the selection. This type of question appears at any grade level. The two examples included are from third and seventh grades, showing opposite ends of the grade-level testing spectrum. Teach students the only way to be absolutely sure of the best answer for the question asked is to *reread* that section of the text.

Game Plan Practice Session

Understanding Questions That Use Facts From the Text as Wrong Answers

Equipment	• Released test passages on overheads • Sample test questions that include facts from the text as wrong answers on overheads • Game plan books • Chart paper and markers or transparency of the strategies
Connection	Team, get your game plan books, it's time for today's game strategy. Today you will learn another secret strategy to unlock test questions. Understanding how answer choices are written helps you to eliminate wrong answers and choose the best answer for each question.

(Continued)

(Continued)

Game strategy: Teaching point	In football, a quarterback may fake a pass to grab the defensive players' attention away from the real action. This is the same in tests. The test writers try to divert your attention from the correct answer choice by including information you have just read as incorrect answer choices. The only way to be sure of the best answer choice is to reread that section of the text.
	(Model by thinking aloud as you work through a couple of examples of questions that have facts from the selection as wrong answer choices. Go through the process of telling students that all of the answers are familiar to you. It is difficult to know which one is correct. They all seem right. Demonstrate how you skim the passage to locate where to look to validate your final choice. For questions, look at the end of the chapter tests in your science or social studies book or use a released passage and questions from your state's test.)
Skill practice: Try it in partnerships	Students, read this short passage. Work in pairs to write a question that uses three facts from the selection as incorrect answer choices, plus the correct answer.
Own it: Independent practice	Using the same passage, now you will independently compose questions that use facts from the selection as incorrect answer choices.
Huddle: Assess and reflect	(Share several questions with the class and have them find the facts that are incorrect answer choices.)
Review game strategy: Link	Remember to be sure the answer you choose answers the question asked.
Closing the session	(In their game plan books, have students record notes about this strategy in their own words.
	If you are charting the strategies, add "*Understanding questions that use facts from the text as wrong answer choices*" to the "Question-Answering Game Strategies" chart.)

Life Skills Connection

All throughout life you will make choices. It is important to be able to sift through facts to make the best choice, whether it is which car to buy or where to have dinner. For example, just because a car looks good on the outside doesn't mean it's a good car for you. When you check out the facts on the car, you may find that it doesn't get good gas mileage or it doesn't come with features that you want.

What other real-life connections can you suggest to help your students see the relevance of this game strategy?

• • •

GAME STRATEGY: UNDERSTANDING "NOT" AND "EXCEPT" QUESTIONS

"Not" and "except" questions require a reversal in thinking from all other questions. Three answer choices contain correct facts from the selection and one contains incorrect information. The test taker looks for the incorrect answer choice for these questions.

Examples

1. *Fourth-Grade Example From 2004–07 California Standards Test Released Items*
   Based on information in the four samples, all of the following words can be used to describe avocado skin *except*

   A. thick
   B. spicy
   C. leathery
   D. rough

Explanation. Students read four short passages on avocados to answer this question. Sample A says "This tree's fruit is oval or pear-shaped and has leathery green, purple or black skin . . ." and sample C states "Its fruit, of the same name, has a thick, rough, greenish skin." The correct answer choice is B, since the other three answer choices accurately describe avocado skin.

2. *Seventh-Grade Example From the Fall 2006 MEAP Released Items*
   According to the selection, Koko's responses express all of the following *except*

   A. creativity
   B. anger
   C. sadness
   D. complex ideas

Explanation. The correct answer is B. In the selection "Going Ape Over Language" by Natalie M. Rosinsky, it clearly states "Both gorillas [Koko and Michael], like Washoe, have shown creativity and logic in naming unknown objects. . . . Koko has also used ASL to express sadness and some complex ideas." Anger is not mentioned.

Game Plan Practice Session

Understanding "Not and Except" Questions

Equipment	• Released test passages on overheads • Sample test "not and except" questions on an overhead • Game plan books • Chart paper and markers or transparency of the strategies
Connection	Team, get your game plan books, it's time for today's game strategy. In past sessions, you learned to choose the correct answer choice to questions. Today will be quite different. You will learn a strategy to help you find the *incorrect* answer.
Game strategy: Teaching point	In "not and except" questions, three answer choices are *correct* facts from the selection and one is *incorrect*. The incorrect answer choice is the one you are looking for. (Demonstrate your thinking. It's best to use a released passage and questions from your state's test. Using the sample questions on the overhead, think aloud each answer choice, determining whether it is true or false. Write a *T* for true or an *F* for false next to each answer choice after going back into the passage, locating the information to confirm your decision. The false answer is the desired answer choice for this type of question.)
Skill practice: Try it in partnerships	Students, read this short passage. With your partners, you read through a "not or except" question. Write a *T* for true or an *F* for false next to each answer choice. The false answer will be the correct choice. Highlight where the information is located in the passage.
Own it: Independent practice	(Have students answer another "not or except" question independently, using the above strategy.)
Huddle: Assess and reflect	(Invite several students to share how they answered this question correctly.)
Review game strategy: Link	Remember, you are looking for the incorrect answer when answering a "not or except" question.
Closing the session	(In their game plan books, have students record notes about this strategy in their own words. If you are charting the strategies, add "*Understanding 'not and except' questions*" to the "Question-Answering Game Strategies" chart.)

GAME STRATEGY: UNDERSTANDING WHAT THE QUESTIONS ASK

Teachers frequently comment, "My students knew that concept well, but still did not get those questions right on the test. Why is that?" Possibly, students did not understand what the question asked. Standardized test questions are written in a formal style of English that is unlike anything else students read or hear (Calkins, Montgomery, Falk, & Santman, 1998).

Think about this. When was the last time you asked your students, "Which one of the following is one central idea of this selection?" You ask about the main idea of selections all of the time, but your language is much less formal. You may ask, "What is this reading about?" This is the language your students are accustomed to hearing and answering.

As teachers, you are good test takers; in fact many of you had to pass a proficiency test to become a teacher. You may not hear the awkwardness of test language. It helps to move this language from the realm of test questions and into a social setting so you can hear the awkwardness. See Figure 3.1 for an example.

Figure 3.1   Script

Setting: Two friends talking after a football game.
Speaker 1   Which of the following <u>best describes</u> today's football game—a miracle or just plain fabulous?!
Speaker 2   I don't know, but it was sure nice to have them win an away game. What <u>characteristic quality</u> do you think our team displayed during the game?
Speaker 1   Discipline!! They played a well-disciplined game, making few mistakes.
Speaker 2   Our special teams played smart by keeping the ball away from their kick returner. On the other hand, did you see the other team's quarterback leave the field? <u>What mood</u> do you think he communicated when he smashed his helmet to the ground?
Speaker 1   Humph! He was *not* happy. He did have a rotten game, but, hey, it happens to everyone. <u>According to</u> the newspaper, he is one of the top quarterbacks in our conference.
Speaker 2   What is <u>one of the *main* reasons</u> for this win?
Speaker 1   Well, our team got really lucky when the field goal attempt that hit the upright bounced over the crossbar and did not bounce back.
Speaker 2   I agree, but I think an <u>important lesson</u> from this game is discipline.
Speaker 1   That may be true but, I think the <u>best summary</u> of this game is a good running game can make the passing game successful.

Because standardized test questions are framed in different terms from what you use in the classroom, students may not understand what the question is asking. In addition, questions ask about the same concept in several different ways, using a variety of unfamiliar terms. You may use the term *conversation* when discussing characters talking in a story in your classroom, but the test uses the term *dialogue*. In math, you might ask for *answers* and the test asks for *sums*, *differences*, *products*, or *quotients*. While you cannot be sure of the exact terminology on the test, you can make students aware of this issue. During daily instruction throughout the year, consciously use the test terms in addition to your usual classroom language. For example, "As you work through these addition problems, circle your answers or sums."

Not only are test questions written in formal English, they also ask students to read and identify information in various ways. Students may have difficulty with the phrasing of a question because they are unfamiliar with the language; therefore, they misunderstand the task. The following examples in this section list alternative phrasing for questions on main idea and author's purpose.

Main Idea Questions

A main idea question may be asked in the following ways:

- What is the selection mostly about?
- What is the selection mainly about?
- Which is the best summary for this selection?
- Which is a good title for this selection?
- Which one of the following is one central idea of this selection?
- Which sentence *best* tells what the story is about?
- What is the main idea of the last paragraph of the article?
- What is the main idea of this selection?

Most of the questions above do not include the term "main idea" in them. Students must understand multiple wordings for main idea questions.

Author's Purpose Questions

Questions about an author's purpose may vary also. The test may ask about the purpose of the entire text or sections of it. Students who can't identify the questions asking about the author's purpose may not be able to answer them correctly, even if they understand the concept of author's purpose. The following examples demonstrate possible wording for author's purpose questions.

Whole Selection Questions for Author's Purpose

- Why did the author include conversation in this selection?
- The central purpose of this selection is to . . .
- The author mainly wrote this selection to . . .
- The central purpose of this selection is to provide . . .
- The author included quotes from the character in this selection *probably* to . . .

Specific Section Questions for Author's Purpose

- Why did the author place a break in the text about halfway through the selection?
- The author uses an exclamation point (!) for the last sentence of the second paragraph of the selection in order to . . .

Most of the above questions on author's purpose do not use the words "author's purpose." Students who understand author's purpose may not recognize that these questions ask about the author's purpose and, therefore, do not answer them correctly.

Vocabulary Questions

Although vocabulary questions are usually more straightforward in their wording, they can become lengthy. Sometimes the length of the question makes it difficult if students do not read the entire question.

Examples

1. *Fifth-Grade Example From the Florida Comprehensive Assessment Test 2005*

   Read these sentences from the story.
   Right in front of me was a new dinosaur! The scientists were putting the bones together. . . . There was a big metal structure all around it for the scientists to climb on.
   What does the word *structure* mean?

2. *Eighth-Grade Example From the Fall 2005 Michigan Education Assessment Program (MEAP) Released Items*

   In paragraph 4, the author wrote that Bentley had "no way to share his enjoyment of the delicate *hexagons.*" Based on the illustration of a snowflake that accompanies the selection, which one of the following is *most likely* the meaning of the word *hexagons?*

Explanation. The examples above demonstrate the possible length of extended vocabulary questions. When the question includes quotes from the text, the question becomes lengthy. Students need reading stamina to read the passages <u>and</u> the questions and answers.

3. *Eighth-Grade Example From the 2004–07 California Standards Test (CST) Released Items*

   Sun Veil Sunscreen provides long-lasting waterproof protection from the sun's <u>burning</u> UVA and UVB rays that will last for a full six hours in or out of water.

   In which sentence does the word <u>burning</u> have the same meaning as in the sentence above?

   A. The <u>burning</u> candle gave off a wonderful scent.
   B. What to have for lunch that day was the <u>burning</u> issue.
   C. Lin had a <u>burning</u> need to know the outcome of the game.
   D. Angeline ran barefoot across the <u>burning</u> pavement.

Explanation. The final question above, while not only lengthy, poses an additional problem. Typically, in a vocabulary question, each answer choice offers a possible definition for the word in question. However, in this question, students are not given possible definitions. Instead, they must find the sentence in which the word has the same meaning as the word in question.

For example, in this question students must understand that the word "burning" in the question means "injury to the skin caused by heat." Then they find the sentence in which burning has the same meaning. Students cannot skim the answers and choose the correct one. They read each answer carefully, decide on the meaning of burning, and make up their minds if it is the same definition as in the sentence given or not before eliminating it. The correct answer is D.

Game Plan Practice Session

Understanding What the Questions Ask

Equipment	<ul><li>Released test passages</li><li>Sample test main idea, author's purpose, and vocabulary questions on overheads</li><li>Copies of the script in Figure 3.1</li><li>Game plan books</li><li>Chart paper and markers or transparency of the strategies</li></ul>
Connection	Team, get your game plan books, it's time for today's game strategy. First let's look at the question-answering strategies you have learned so far: Understanding questions that have "almost right" answers Understanding questions that use facts from the text as wrong answers Understanding "not and except" questions You certainly are becoming masters of test taking! Today you will learn the last game strategy for answering test questions, which is identifying what a question is asking. I bet there were times when you read a test question and said "Huh? What does that mean?" Today you will learn how to read a test question and understand what it is asking you to think and do.
Game strategy: Teaching point	Test makers write standardized test questions in formal English or test language, unlike anything else you read or hear. They use ordinary words, but they are put together into awkward phrases we rarely see. For example, it would be unusual for me to ask you, "Which one of the following is one central idea of this selection?" You would scratch your heads and wonder what I was talking about. However, if I asked you, "What is this story about?" you would understand what I wanted from you. In baseball, the third base coach uses secret hand signals to provide instructions to the batter and the base runners regarding the next pitch. The team members must learn what those signals mean. The same goes for test-taking skills. Good test takers can look at a question and figure out what they are asked to do, even if it is not said specifically. Not only do test makers write questions in very formal English, they also ask about a concept that you really do know, but they may ask about it in several different ways. It is important to be able to understand what the questions ask. (Present students with released test questions. Review a variety of questions on the overheads showing students how you know if it is a main idea, author's purpose, or vocabulary question. Look at the variety of wording for each. What words clued you into what kind of a question it is?)

(Continued)

(Continued)

Skill practice: Try it in partnerships	Partners, read this script. Highlight and discuss the phrases that sound awkward to you. Rewrite them into more familiar terms. (Have partners share the rewrites.)
Own it: Independent practice	Now that you have thought about the awkward phrasing of questions, think about the clues I showed you earlier to help you recognize different questions. I want you to read these questions and decide if they are main idea, author's purpose, or vocabulary questions. (Using a page of a sample test items, have students find examples of main idea, author's purpose, and vocabulary questions. Look at the wording and talk about how they will recognize these questions on a test.)
Huddle: Assess and reflect	(Have students get in groups of three or four. Students read one of their questions aloud. The other students tell what type of question it is and explain how they identified it.)
Review game strategy: Link	Remember, to answer a question correctly, you must understand what it is asking. Test makers may ask about the same concept in a number of different ways.
Closing the session	(In their game plan books, have students record notes about this strategy in their own words. If you are charting the strategies, add "Understanding what the question is asking" to the "Question-Answering Game Strategies" chart.)

Life Skills Connection

Learning to read and answer questions thoughtfully will be helpful when taking driver's tests, college entrance exams, professional certification exams, and completing employment questionnaires.

What other real-life connections can you suggest to help your students see the relevance of this game strategy?

• • •

Question-Answering Game Strategies

- Understanding questions that have "almost right" answers
- Understanding questions that use facts from the text as wrong answer choices
- Understanding "not and except" questions
- Understanding what the questions ask

ASSESSMENT

Using released items from your state test or the chapter test from a content area textbook, give students a practice test composed of about six questions. Try to use questions that demonstrate the various types you taught your students. While students work, circulate around the classroom, lean in over their shoulders and ask why they chose a certain answer or how they eliminated other choices. Watch for patterns. What is the specific distractor for which they are falling? This provides the information you need for further review.

To encourage metacognition, explain how to complete Figure 3.2, Question-Answering Checklist, on page 69. Students will complete this checklist immediately after taking the practice test and before scoring it. The checklist encourages students to become aware of how they handle certain questions. It may not be appropriate for younger students.

> ### TIME-OUT
>
> ### What kind of questions are on your state test?
>
> To focus your teaching, study your state test. Pay attention to your thinking as you answer test questions. As the test expert, your students count on you to coach them on game sense or test sense. Test sense requires that you make your thinking visible so students can use your model as a guide to their thinking on the test.
>
> 1. Are the questions and answers similar to the types of questions included here?
>
> 2. If not, how do they vary?

Have students score their answers. Model how to identify strengths and weakness by combining test performance with test strategy use. Ask students to turn to a partner to identify their strengths and weaknesses. They will discuss which questions they could answer correctly and those with which they struggled as well as the question-answering game strategies that helped them during this practice round. Next, they will set goals for a future test performance and a second practice round.

FINAL THOUGHTS

As tests increasingly become gatekeepers to employment opportunities, these strategies provide equal opportunities for all students. While directed toward the third- through eighth-grade tests, these strategies apply to many other standardized tests.

Some students take test preparation classes offered by local or county-wide school districts. Others pay to attend test preparation classes that are focused to raise achievement on a particular test. When students know and own game strategies, the playing field is leveled for them. They deserve no less.

Figure 3.2   Question-Answering Checklist

I Found	I Remembered to (Sample Student Comments)
Questions with "almost right" answers	I went back and reread that part of the selection. I refigured the problem.
Questions that use facts from the text as wrong answers	I went back to the selection and looked up the facts.
"Not and except" questions	I wrote true or false by each answer. I marked the false answer on the answer sheet.
Main idea, author's purpose, and vocabulary questions	I asked myself, "What is this question asking?"

Constructed Response Questions

Empirical research has determined that students' ability to process and remember informational text is correlated with ability to recognize text structures.

—José Montelongo and Anita Hernandez (2007, p. 540)

GAME STRATEGY FOR STUDENTS

Understand That . . .

- Writing a quality response to a question requires the writer to use good reading skills, analyze questions, and write clear and thoughtful responses.

Know

- Types of constructed response questions (CRQ)

Able to Do

- Analyze a constructed response question, determine what it is asking them to do, and write a quality response with supporting details

PREPARING TO ANSWER CONSTRUCTED RESPONSE QUESTIONS

Not all state tests have constructed response questions, so if your state's test does not include them, you may wish to skip this chapter. However, since information from this chapter will *definitely* help students in all subject area coursework and in life beyond school, you may choose to teach this at another time.

After explaining to students what a constructed response question is, there are three strategies that students will need to know in order to respond well to constructed response questions. First of all, students must be able to identify what the question is asking them to do. Next, they will need to determine if the answer to the question is in the text (literal) or in their head (inferential). Finally, they will need to compose a quality response that addresses the question and gives details to support their ideas.

GAME STRATEGY: DETERMINING THE TEXT STRUCTURE OF A QUESTION

As you begin the lessons on constructed response questions, explain to students that a constructed response question comes after reading a passage, after looking at a chart or graph, or after a mathematical problem is presented. So to answer the question effectively, they must first carefully read the information in the question.

Next explain that to respond to a constructed response question, the test taker has to create or construct a response or answer in writing. Constructed response questions may require answers that are a few words or answers that are several sentences depending on the question. So for these questions, they will not fill in dots or circles from a choice of responses; they will read the question and use key information from the text or in their head to create and write their response.

Next students need to review expository text structures. In this first game strategy, students look at questions to determine the text structure of the question. They will need to know the expository text structures discussed in Chapter 2. Knowledge of text structure helps them know how to construct their response. The chart below reviews the structures and offers clues they may see in the questions that help them know how to answer the question. As you are modeling with the students and as students are practicing, you would refer back to this chart. Please note that we have broken this section into four lessons. If you are working with third- to fourth-grade students, you will probably want to do these as separate lessons. Teachers in Grades 5 through 8 may feel they can combine the first three lessons into one. You will need to decide what works best for your students.

TIME-OUT

What kind of constructed response questions are on your state test?

To focus your teaching, study your state test and identify the text structure of the constructed response questions. Think about how you would answer those questions based on the text structure.

Figure 4.1   Expository Questions Chart

Text Structure	Definition	Question Clues
Description	Information gives visual details	The question may ask you to describe something or someone with examples.
Sequential	Information presented in chronological order from beginning to end	The question may ask you to tell the order in which something happens, or show a step-by-step process.
Compare and contrast	Information shows how two or more items are alike and different	The question may ask you to tell or explain how things are the same or different, or compare and contrast something.
Problem-solution	Information poses a problem and possible solution	The question may ask you to explain what the problem is and how you would solve it, or give you the problem and ask you for the solution.
Cause and effect	Information explains why something happened	The question may ask you to give the reason for, explain what will happen if, explain what causes this, explain the effect of this, or explain how this does. . . .

Game Plan Practice Session

Determining the Text Structure of a Question

Equipment	• Several constructed response questions from your state test or several questions with varying text structures from a textbook you use with your students • Game plan books • Chart paper to make a chart as you teach the game strategies in this unit
Connection	Test takers, are you ready to learn some new strategies for test taking? The game strategies you learn in the next few days will help you in your classes, in college, and in life, for example, in getting a job! Since we have already talked about what a constructed response question (CRQ) is, now we are going to use our knowledge of expository text structure to help us know how we should respond to that type of test question.
Game strategy: Teaching point	In sports such as football or basketball, there are key words that all players use that help them know what kind of moves to make in the game. For example, in football, all players know that *huddle* means to gather together to discuss a play. Or in basketball, when they hear *free throw* they all know where to move into position on the court. Well, just like in most sports, CRQs have clue words in them that help a test taker know how to respond. We're going to practice learning to find those clue words that will help us answer the question. Students, all CRQs are expository questions even if they are related to narrative text, so you will need to read and analyze the questions to look for clue words that help you find the expository text structure of the question. Let's review what we know about text structures. Notice how this new chart has not only the text structures in it, but also has clues to help us figure out the text structure in the questions. We will see how we can use this knowledge to write our responses. Now I am going to share some sample questions with you, and then I will show you how I identify the text structure of the question. (Teachers, for the game strategies in this chapter, you will find examples of test questions and think-alouds; however, remember it's best to use examples from released items from your state test or a content area test.) Example Test Question and Teacher Think-Aloud *1. Fifth-Grade Example From 2006 Michigan Educational Assessment Program Released Items* *In some places, scientists locate elephants by using an electronic tracking device. This method involves putting a collar containing the device on the elephant so that the elephant's position can be tracked.* **Describe** *two benefits of using electronic tracking technology on the elephants.* **Describe** *one risk to the elephants if this system is used.* Explanation: I notice that both of these questions use the word *describe* in them. That means that my answer needs to be a response that gives a clear *description* with supporting details.

Skill practice: Try it in partnerships	Class, now I'd like you to read a few sample questions from the state-released CRQs (or from your textbook) with a partner. With your team partner, see if you can identify the text structures of these questions. (Next have the whole class share and discuss the structure of the question. Also have students note key words that helped them see the text structure, e.g., words and phrases like *compare, describe, the causes,* etc.)
	Example and Student Think-Aloud
	Fourth-Grade Example From 2005 Michigan Educational Assessment Program Released Items
	Problem-Solution/Description
	Allison is buying fish for her brothers and sisters. Allison has 3 brothers and one sister. She wants to buy 3 fish for each.
	Part A: Explain how Allison can determine the number of fish she needs to buy.
	Part B: Write a number sentence that can be used to determine the number of fish Allison needs to buy.
	Part C: How many fish does Allison need to buy?
	Student Explanation: I notice that this is a story problem. I am supposed to do three things in my answer to this problem. First, I need to explain how Alison can determine the number of fish, then I need to write a number sentence, then I need to solve the problem by telling how many fish she needs to buy. Because I have to find an answer, I think this is mostly a problem-solution question, but I also need to do some describing in words and in numbers to show my thinking about how to solve the problem.
Own it: Independent practice	Students, now I would like you to try to identify the structure of a few questions on your own.
	Example and Student Think-Aloud
	Eighth Grade Example From 2004 New York Regents Exam Released Items
	Cause and Effect: Whales have a thick layer of blubber (fat) under their skin. How does this layer of blubber help whales to maintain a constant body temperature?
	Explanation: I know that cause-and-effect questions work like this question. I am thinking of the because/then statements that show cause and effect and I think that works for this one. Because the whale has blubber then. . . . Yes, I think that will help me get to the answer for this question.
Huddle: Assess and reflect	(Have students share their findings with the class. Be sure to include talk about the clues they used to help them think about what the question might be asking them to do.)

(Continued)

(Continued)

Review game strategy: Link	Remember, just like team players know what to do when they hear certain words, effective test takers use their knowledge of expository text structure to help know what a CRQ is asking them to do.
	You will find that knowledge of text structure will help you answer questions in all your classes, in college, and in life. Once I learned to recognize text structures, I could see them everywhere—in newspaper articles, magazines, books I was reading. It was cool to have this shared knowledge with the author, and it helped me make sense of the text.
Closing the session	(In their game plan books, have students record notes about this strategy in their own words.
	If you are charting, create a chart titled "Constructed Response Question Game Strategies" and record *"Read the question and determine the text structure of the question"* as the first strategy.)

Life Skills Connection

It's true: Once you become aware of varying text structures, you will start to see them everywhere. Next time you read a newspaper or magazine article, note the text structures within the article. You should find that most articles use several text structures.

What other real-life connections can you suggest to help your students see the relevance of this game strategy?

• • •

GAME STRATEGY: LITERAL OR INFERENTIAL RESPONSES

In this lesson, students learn that sometimes they will find the answer to a constructed response question within the text, chart or graph, or problem that precedes the question, and sometimes the answer must be inferred and come from their own thoughts.

Game Plan Practice Session

Literal or Inferential Responses

Equipment	• The same passages that you used in the previous lesson from either your state test or textbook. • Game plan books • Chart for charting new strategy
Connection	Students, we have reviewed expository text structures, and we practiced identifying the structure of CRQs. Today, we will learn to identify whether the answers to these questions are in the text (point to the text) or if the answer is in our heads and not in the text (point to your head). Oftentimes in sports, players use hand signals to help them communicate with each other. Today, we will use hand signals to show when we think the answer is in the text (point to the text) or if it is in our heads (point to your head). (Throughout this lesson, continue to point to the text or at your head as needed. Movement helps students cement the learning!)
Game strategy: Teaching point	If I know what the question is asking me to do (compare or contrast, etc.), and I carefully read the text related to the passage, I should be able to determine where I find the answer—in the text or in my head. If an answer is in the text, it is called a literal response; that means I can use exact words from the text in my answer. If the answer is in my head, it is called an inferential response, which means I looked at evidence from the text and my own reasoning skills and came up with my own answer in my head. Let me share an example with you. Here's the same passage I used in the last strategy. Let me read it again. Example and Teacher Think Aloud: *In some places, scientists locate elephants by using an electronic tracking device. This method involves putting a collar containing the device on the elephant so that the elephant's position can be tracked.* **Describe** *two benefits of using electronic tracking technology on the elephants.* **Describe** *one risk to the elephants if this system is used.* Explanation: I recall that I need to write a response that describes. Now I need to see if the answer to this question is in the text or in my head. (Skim through the text looking for the answer.) Hmmm, I don't see anything in this text that answers the question. That means I have to infer or find the answer in my head. Okay, when I get ready to write this answer, I have to see if I can get some information from the text and then the rest must come from in my head.

(Continued)

(Continued)

Skill practice: Try it in partnerships	With your partners, look back at the questions you studied while learning the previous strategy and decide if the answer is in the text or in your head. When I ask you where the answer is, either point to the text or point to your head depending on where you think the answer is.
	Example and Student Think-Aloud:
	Fourth-Grade Example From 2005 Michigan Educational Assessment Program Released Items
	Problem-Solution/Description
	Allison is buying fish for her brothers and sisters. Allison has 3 brothers and one sister. She wants to buy 3 fish for each.
	Part A: Explain how Allison can determine the number of fish she needs to buy.
	Part B: Write a number sentence that can be used to determine the number of fish Allison needs to buy.
	Part C: How many fish does Allison need to buy?
	Explanation: I recall that I need to write a response that describes and shows a solution to the problem. Now I need to see if the answer to this question is in the text or in my head. (Skim through the text looking for the answer.) Hmmm, I can get some information for the answer in the text, like the number of brothers and sisters Alison has and the number of fish she wants to buy for each. But I am going to have to figure out how to solve the problem in my head. Okay, when I get ready to write this answer, I know I can get some information from the text and then the rest must come from in my head.
Own it: Independent practice	Now, students, it's time to try this on your own. Looking at these next passages, decide if the answers to these questions are in the text or in your head. Don't forget to point to where the answer is!
	Example and Student Think-Aloud:
	Eighth Grade Example From 2004 New York Regents Exam Released Items
	Cause and Effect: Whales have a thick layer of blubber (fat) under their skin. How does this layer of blubber help whales to maintain a constant body temperature?
	Explanation: I recall that I need to write a response that shows cause and effect. Now I need to see if the answer to this question is in the text or in my head. (Skim through the text looking for the answer.) Hmmm, there's not much in the text to help me answer this question, so I am going to have to figure out how to answer it in my head using what I know about whales and blubber.

Huddle: Assess and reflect	(Have students share and compare their decisions with a partner then discuss any discrepancies with the whole class. Next have students discuss other places in school and in life where they might be able to use this strategy to answer questions.)
Review game strategy: Link	Remember that good test takers determine whether the answer to a CRQ is in the text or in their head.
Closing the session	(In their game plan books, have students record notes about this strategy in their own words. If you are charting, add *"Determine if the answer to the question is in the text (literal) or in your head (inferential)"* to the "Constructed Response Question Game Strategies" chart.)

Life Skills Connection

Throughout life, when effective readers have to respond to questions related to text, they automatically ask themselves, "Do I know this answer already, or can I find the answer in the text?"

What other real-life connections can you suggest to help your students see the relevance of this game strategy?

• • •

GAME STRATEGY: WRITING A QUALITY RESPONSE

Once test takers have read the text (or chart, graph, or map), read the constructed response question noting the text structure of the question, and determined whether the answer to the question is in the text or in their head, they must learn to write the answers to the questions. It is important that teachers model how they think to construct an effective response.

Example of a Think-Aloud for Writing an Answer to a Constructed Response Question

Let me think aloud and show you how I would write the response to the question I analyzed yesterday. (The teacher models the writing of the response on the overhead or SMART Board, saying aloud her thought processes as she writes.)

(Continued)

(Continued)

First, when I look at the space in the test booklet for answering this question (show the test booklet to students), I see there are about eight lines for me to write on, so that means I should write the answer in a complete sentence.

Next, I am going to reread the question: *"In some places scientists locate elephants by using an electronic tracking device. This method involves putting a collar containing the device on the elephant so that the elephant's position can be tracked.* **Describe** *two benefits of using electronic tracking technology on the elephants.* **Describe** *one risk to the elephants if this system is used."*

Now, I see that the answer to this question is not in the text; it is in my head. I need to think of two benefits and one risk to the elephants. Benefits . . . let me see . . . I think that we could learn more about the elephants if we tag them, then we can help them more. And if they are in trouble or having problems, we will be able to find them and help them. A risk would be . . . well . . . maybe the collar would get stuck on something out in the jungle and the animal would get hurt.

I am ready to write the answer. I need to be sure to add specific descriptive details and write the answer in a complete sentence.

The benefits of tagging the elephants would be that we would be able to learn more about them so we can help them, and we would be able to get to them if they need help. One of the risks of tagging the elephants is that the collar could get stuck in something in the jungle and the elephant would be trapped.

In rereading this and checking on the rubric, I see that my response includes specific text structure knowledge, I embedded the question in the answer, and my response includes thorough examples and details. According to the rubric, I have done a very thorough job on my response.

Game Plan Practice Session

Writing a Quality Response

Equipment	• Equipment to project your writing for the students to see (overhead, SMART Board, document camera) • Several test questions from your state test • Sample test response booklet • Game plan books • Chart for charting new strategy

Connection	In a football game, players huddle, plan the play, signal each other, and then what do they do? (Run the play!) Yes, the final step is to play the game. Grades 5–8: So now it's time for us to play the game and write the answers to the CRQs we have been analyzing. Grades 3–4: Are you ready for the next strategy, test takers? You have learned to carefully read the text passage, analyze the question to determine the text structure, and decide whether the answer to the question is in the text or in your heads. What do you suspect strategic test takers need to do next? (Call on someone.) Write the answer to the question? How many of you agree with that? Yes, it's time to learn to write quality answers.
Game strategy: Teaching point	Just like when football players run the play, they follow predetermined plans, when I create my written response to a CRQ, there are three things I do. I look at how much space is given for the answer. This lets me know how long the answer is expected to be. Once I have determined the text structure and whether the answer is in the text or in my head, I plan to use specific examples and details in my answer. If the space indicates or directions say that the answer requires more than a one- or two-word response, I repeat the question by embedding it in the answer to create a complete sentence. Let me think aloud and show you how I would write the response to the question I analyzed yesterday. (Teacher, model the writing of the response on the overhead or SMART Board, saying aloud your thought processes as you write. See an example of this think-aloud on pages 79–80.)
Skill practice: Try it in partnerships	Now I would like you to work with your partners to write a good response to the question you analyzed yesterday. (Have students work with their partners and write a complete and correct answer together. Have students share their answers with the whole class and discuss any questions or concerns.)
Own it: Independent practice	Now, students, you will try writing a response on your own to the question you worked on earlier. (Have students write their own responses while you float around the room asking questions and supporting as needed.)

(Continued)

(Continued)

Huddle: Assess and reflect	(Have students share their varied written responses. Together they note which answers are quality, thorough responses.)
Review game strategy: Link	Remember, like football players who plan plays to win games, you have strategies to write an answer to a CRQ. You will do three things: (1) notice how long your answer needs to be, (2) use specific details and examples in your answer, and (3) embed the question in your answer.
Closing the session	Students, in your game plan books, bullet these three points about this strategy. (If you are charting, add *"(1) notice how long your answer needs to be, (2) use specific details and examples in your answer, and (3) embed the question in your answer"* to the "Constructed Response Questions Game Strategies" chart.)

———— Life Skills Connection ————

Job applications often include constructed response questions. Students who take the constructed response strategies they learn into the world with them will have a better chance of getting the job.

Examples

When asked to give your work or education history, you would write the answer in sequential order. If you didn't bring your history with you on a resume (which would make it an easy "in the text" answer to write), you have to try to recall the timeline "in your head." It pays to be prepared.

When asked to describe any special talents, interests, or hobbies, you know to respond using descriptive words, so rather than simply saying, "I like to hike," you might add some detail such as, "My goal is to hike in every continent by the time I am ___." This detailed description will give you a jump on the applicant who just lists hobbies rather than gives specific details and examples.

What other real-life connections can you suggest to help your students see the relevance of this game strategy?

● ● ●

GAME STRATEGY: MEMORIZE THE RESCUE STRATEGY

Teachers often complain that students can utilize procedures or strategies when they are in class; however, many do not implement them independently.

The following mnemonic is designed to assist students in remembering and using the multistep procedure to respond to a CRQ taught over the last several days. The mnemonic is RESCUE. In this final practice session, you will have students memorize the RESCUE strategy using a technique called rapid fire verbal rehearsal.

Figure 4.2   RESCUE

A Strategy for Responding to "Constructed Response Questions"	
Read	the question carefully and thoroughly.
Examine	the question and determine the expository text type (look for *clue* words in the question).
Skim	the text again.
Choose	whether the answer is in the text (literal) or in your head (inferential).
Use	specific details and examples in your answer.
Embed	the question in your answer (complete sentences).

Game Plan Practice Session

Memorize the RESCUE Strategy

Equipment	• RESCUE strategy on overhead or PowerPoint slide • Overhead or LCD player • Pointer (optional, but fun for using during rapid fire verbal rehearsal)
Connection	Okay, students, here's the last game plan strategy we are going to learn for CRQ, and it's a fun one!
Game strategy: Teaching point	Since there are several steps you need to use to respond to a constructed response question, I am going to teach you a mnemonic that will help you remember the steps we have learned. It's called the RESCUE strategy. (Show the students an overhead or PowerPoint slide of the strategy.) I am going to show you how fast you can memorize this strategy using a really fun memorization strategy called rapid fire verbal rehearsal. Be prepared! Everyone will be called on as we do this, so be ready to respond when I point to you. I am going to put the steps of the strategy up for you to see. (Teacher, put up an overhead or PowerPoint slide with the steps of the RESCUE strategy.) Next, I am going to point to someone in the room and they have to say just one step of the strategy. So the first person would start by saying, "Read the question thoroughly and carefully." The next person will say, "Examine the question and notice the text structure," and so on. I will keep going around the room over and over again, and each of you will be called on to say a step of the strategy. After we have done this for awhile, I will start to remove some of the prompts so you can start to memorize the strategy. This will get more challenging, but don't worry, you will be able to get help from me or someone else if you don't have all the steps down when you are called on. We are learning this together and you will have lots of practice. (*Round One:* Go around the room and call on all the students to say a step of the strategy. *Round Two:* Once they start to catch on, scaffold by removing all but the key word in the prompt: Read, Examine, Skim, Choose, Use, Embed. Now go around the room again calling on students. They must explain the whole step of the strategy, not just say the key word. *Round Three:* Once they get good at this, take away all but the first initial of each step: R, E, S, C, U, E. Go around the room again until you can see that students are starting to know the strategy without the prompts.)

Skill practice: Try it in partnerships	Now, I would like you to get with your partner and take turns saying the steps of the strategy. When you think you have it, call me over, and I will listen to you both say the steps together.
Own it: Independent practice	Okay, students, ultimately you will be on your own when you take the test and respond to CRQs. If you own this strategy, you will have a great tool for helping you break down the steps that will help you write a quality response, not just on the test but whenever you have to answer CRQs. In your head, practice saying the steps of the strategy and see if you have them. Keep trying until you know you've got it!
Huddle: Assess and reflect	I am going to give you a copy of the RESCUE strategy to glue into your game plan books, so you know where it is if you need to practice. After you have glued it in, please write why this strategy is important for you to know and use. (If you are charting, add *"Knowing the RESCUE strategy will give you a tool for recalling how to write a response to a CRQ"* to the "Constructed Response Question Game Strategies" chart.)
Review game strategy: Link	How many of you have a trick that helps you do something successfully? (Students share tricks they use.) Remember, when you learn a mnemonic like RESCUE, it helps you have a game plan tool at your side when you go to take a test.
Closing the session	One more time, let's all say the steps of the RESCUE strategy together. After we have said the last step, I want everyone to jump up and high five their partners and say, "We are AWESOME test takers! Yes!"

Life Skills Connection

Throughout our lives, we use memory tricks to help us. I wrote my own vows for my wedding. If ever there was a time I was going to be nervous, I knew it would be at the altar. I made up word clues that helped me remember key parts of my vows, then I practiced saying them over and over again, using the key words as a trigger to help me. Needless to say, despite my nervousness, I did just fine!

Outside of the classroom, students may have to find tricks to memorize something for a school play, club or group, or religious ceremony.

What other real-life connections can you suggest to help your students see the relevance of this game strategy?

• • •

> ### Constructed Response
> ### Questions Game Strategies
>
> - Read the question and determine the text structure of the question.
> - Determine if the answer to the question is in the text (literal) or in your head (inferential).
> - When writing your response to a CRQ do the following:
>   - Note the space or lines in the test packet. That helps you know how long your answer is expected to be.
>   - Use specific details and examples in your answer.
>   - If the answer is longer than one or two words, embed the question in your answer.
> - Knowing the RESCUE strategy will give you a tool for recalling how to write a response to a CRQ.

ASSESSMENT

Using released constructed response items from your state test, constructed response questions from a content area textbook, or CRQs of your own design, give students several to practice. Try to use questions that demonstrate the various text structures you have taught your students. Have students score answers on a rubric (see Figure 4.3, a sample rubric). Discuss how they scored each other's responses and how they can improve their responses.

FINAL THOUGHTS

Research by Dickson, Simmons, and Kame'enui (1998) states, "Text structure appears to play an important role in reading comprehension" (p. 17). Teaching students the text structures that writers use and showing them how to organize that material positively impacts comprehension (Dymock, 2005, p. 178).

The research clearly indicates that teaching students strategies for responding to constructed response questions on a test will be of great use to them not only while taking a test but also when they are answering questions throughout their schooling and in their lives outside of school.

Figure 4.3   Rubric for Scoring Constructed Response Questions

Score Point	Expectations
3	The response includes specific text structure knowledge; if more than one or two words, the question is embedded in the answer; the writer's response was thorough including specific examples and details.
2	The response seems to indicate text structure knowledge; if more than one or two words, the question is embedded in the answer; the writer's response was thorough.
1	The response does not connect to the text structure of the question and the question is not embedded in the answer.
0	The response is incorrect.

Writing to a Prompt

The reason a writer composes a text is to communicate meaning to his intended audience. For this reason, meaning isn't just one of the many qualities of good writing we consider when we assess whether or not a text is well written; meaning is the most important of the traits.

—Carl Anderson (2005, p. 58)

GAME STRATEGY FOR STUDENTS

Understand That . . .

- Writing a quality response to a prompt requires both reading and writing skills to analyze the prompt, to plan and craft the response, and to analyze the written response, checking for clarity to meet the expectations of the test rubric.

Know

- Formats and types of prompt writing questions
- Organizational patterns of response for prompt writing questions

Able to Do

- Analyze an on-demand prompt; plan, organize, and write a quality response with supporting details; write consciously, assessing the writing and adjusting it to meet the expectations of the test rubric

CONSCIOUS PLANNING AND WRITING

Not all state tests have on-demand writing questions that ask students to write to a prompt. If your state's test does not include them, you may wish to skip this chapter. However, since information from this chapter will *definitely* help students in all subject area coursework and in life beyond school, you may choose to teach these game strategies at another time.

Think of writing to a prompt as a unique genre. Similar to other types of writing, prompts ask students to illustrate, explain, inform, persuade, describe, or tell about a time. Unlike other genres and writing settings, students write a response directly connected to a prompt. Often the prompt or a rubric explicitly states the structure or qualities expected. The response is generally written head-to-pen without sufficient time, ownership, or response from other writers. Therefore, being familiar with the prompt, the task, and the rubric is essential for success. Gere, Christenbury, and Sassi (2005), in *Writing on Demand: Best Practices and Strategies for Success,* suggest students are able to know the difference between rich writing that takes weeks to write and limited writing accomplished in a test setting that is controlled by the prompt. Therefore, teaching students how to write for a variety of purposes and a variety of audiences throughout the year enables them to transfer their knowledge about quality writing and consciously make adjustments for the test setting.

As you prepare yourself to help students write to a prompt, review your state test. Study the test and write responses to a variety of prompts. Be metacognitive—think about your own planning and writing process. Understanding the format and expectations of the prompt is key to a successful response. Identify the consistent parts of your prompts. The two examples that follow demonstrate the consistent parts and the explicit and implicit expectations of the prompt. Also review rubrics or checklists that further define the expectations. As the expert test taker, you are coaching your students on how to think while they independently take the test.

Examples

1. *Third-Grade Example From 2004 Colorado State Assessment Program Released Test Items—CSAP Writing*

Consistent Parts	Released Test Example
(1) Topic (2) Length/organization (3) Content—two-part response	What makes you (1) <u>happy</u>? Write a (2) <u>paragraph</u> in which you (2) <u>describe</u> (3) <u>something that makes you happy</u> and (2) <u>explain</u> why it makes you happy.

Explanation. This brief prompt used on the CSAP writing has three parts: topic, length, and content. Although it is brief, the first sentence explicitly states the topic (*being happy*). The second sentence states three important pieces: length (*a paragraph*), organization (*describe*), and content (*something that makes you happy* and *explain why it makes you happy*). Students can write a narrative or expository paragraph. The length and organization are explicit. By stating *paragraph*, the readers (scorers) might expect to see a traditionally structured paragraph with a topic and a concluding sentence.

2. *Eighth-Grade Example From 2007 Florida Comprehensive Assessment Test Released Items—Writing+*

Consistent Parts	Released Test Example
(1) Topic (2) Content (3) Organization	(1) Most <u>teenagers have chores</u>. (2) Think about <u>why it is important</u> for teenagers to have chores. (3) Now write to <u>explain why it is important</u> for teenagers to have chores.

Explanation. This prompt announces the topic (*teenagers have chores*) in a statement. The next two sentences direct the reader to think about and then write to explain the content (*why it is important for teenagers to have chores*). The organization (*explain*) and purpose (*why it is important*) suggest that an expository paragraph or essay will effectively answer the prompt. However, a focused narrative could also illustrate why it is important to have chores. The length is not explicitly stated. Is a paragraph enough? Advise students by looking at the rubric, released student samples, or the paper used during the test.

TIME-OUT

What prompted writing questions are on your state test?

With a partner, review prompts from your test. Look at prompts from multiple years to identify the consistent demands. After identifying the challenges and expectations of your test, select the appropriate game plan strategies.

Format

1. What is the format of the prompt? What are the consistent parts?

2. What topics or big ideas are frequently in the released prompts?

(Continued)

(Continued)

Length and Organization

1. What length, genre, or organizational patterns are expected?
2. Does the prompt or rubric provide explicit or implicit expectations?

Content and Process

1. Does the prompt, rubric, or scored release samples provide explicit or implicit expectations?
2. How much time is allotted for the writing? Will students have time to revise or edit? Is revision or editing expected?

GAME STRATEGY: IDENTIFY THE TOPIC AND STRUCTURE— LIFT KEY WORDS

As you begin the lessons on writing to a prompt, explain to students what they can probably expect to be the same and what might change. In most prompts, the topic, length, or writing structure will change. Explain the scoring criteria on the rubric and show examples of exemplary pieces. Keep the expectations list short and focused to avoid overwhelming the students. If they know the prompt format and what scorers expect, they can use this knowledge to identify the topic, length or organization, and the content of the response.

Next explain that unlike other test questions, there may not be a correct answer. Instead the scorers are evaluating the writer's ability to construct and write a response related to the prompt.

The most common text structures used in writing to a prompt are listed in Figure 5.1.

Figure 5.1 Basic Test Writing Structures

Text Structure	Definition	Question Clues
Narrative: Personal or fiction	A story that illustrates a point or describes an event, generally told in sequence or chronological order.	The question may ask you to • write a narrative • tell about a time • illustrate an event • describe a time
Expository or informational	A paragraph or essay that explains, illustrates, or describes a person, place, event, or idea. The writing is supported with examples, reasons, or facts.	The question may ask you to • explain • illustrate • describe • state the causes • state the effects • compare or contrast

Game Plan Practice Session

Identify the Topic and Structure—Lift Key Words

Equipment	• Released writing to a prompt questions (three different questions) • Game plan books • Chart paper and markers
Connection	Test takers, over the next few days you are going to plan and use game strategies to write to a prompt. As you do this, you will recall what you know about the format and the expectations of a scorer for this prompt. You will also carefully read the prompt to identify what the prompt is asking you to do, what the topic is, and the length or organization a scorer is expecting to see in your response. So let's get started with the first game strategy.
Game strategy: Teaching point	If I said "inning," you would immediately think of baseball. If I said "period," you would immediately think of hockey. If I said "rounds," you would think of golf. Each sport has language that defines how you play it. A baseball or hockey player, like a golfer, knows what to expect and how to play depending on the inning, period, or round in a game.
	Effective test takers step into the test knowing how the test works. Effective test takers know the question format will be consistent in these ways. Your test has these consistent parts: (state the ways).
	In addition, test takers know they have to be careful readers to identify key words that focus the topic and length or organization of the writing as well as the content. They also know they will use this information to decide what to write about and how to write it. You know these things because you have seen this type of prompt before. So let's begin by naming the parts that are consistent. (Using an overhead of the on-demand prompt, highlight, name, and label the consistent parts of the question.)
	Now, let me show you how I think as I read and analyze a prompt. First, I identify the words that state the topic. (Underline exact words.) Later, I will lift these words out of the test question and use these words in my written response.
	Next, I identify the words that state or suggest the length or organization I will use to plan and write the response. (Underline exact words. Explain what these words state or suggest and how this will impact your planning. Explain how the language in the prompt also explicitly or implicitly states the criteria or scorer's expectations.)
	Let's confirm what I know. I know the topic (point to and repeat the topic). I know the genre and length or organization (point to and repeat the key words). The last job is to write a sentence that uses these key words and states the focus and the purpose of my response.
	(Model writing a sentence that restates the prompt and focuses the purpose of a response. Be sure to include the key words from the question. This sentence focuses the planning process.)

(Continued)

(Continued)

Skill practice: Try it in partnerships	Now I am going to give you a new prompt to try the same thinking and reading I just showed you. With your teammates, carefully highlight and select the exact words that state the topic of your response. Be sure to highlight any words that help you focus your response. In addition, highlight the clue words that indicate the length of your response and how your response will be organized. When you have done this, collaboratively write a sentence that restates the prompt and focuses the purpose of a response. Be sure to include the key words from the prompt.
Own it: Independent practice	Now it's time to try this on your own. Independently, do this same thinking as you carefully read, highlight, and select exact words that help focus your response on another new prompt. Independently write a sentence that restates the prompt and focuses the purpose of a response. Be sure to include the key words from the prompt.
Huddle: Assess and reflect	Before we reflect on this strategy, turn and share your work with a partner. You will do three things: (1) Notice if you selected the same key words. Discuss why those words are helpful or essential. If you discovered you selected different words, determine why you might have made different choices, but then come to consensus on the words that are most essential and helpful to focus a response. (2) Compare the sentences that you wrote that helped you focus the response. Identify the key words in the sentence. If necessary, revise these sentences. (3) Select which sentence most effectively restates the prompt and focuses the response. Be prepared to read the sentence you wrote and explain why it is effective. (As students compare their independent practice with a partner, listen to assess your students' thinking. Note any new thinking students did in this very focused reading and thinking activity.)
Review game strategy: Link	Good test takers study the prompt carefully to focus their writing. Using what you know about the format to identify the key words in the prompt will focus the decisions you make as you plan and write.
Closing the session	In your game plan books, do the following: 1. Start a new page and write today's game strategy at the top. 2. Then write three to five sentences explaining the strategy. 3. List the steps you used to read, think, identify, and then write a focused sentence that restates the prompt and states the purpose for a response. (If you are charting, create a chart entitled "Writing to a Prompt Game Strategies" and record *"Identifying the topic and structure—lift key words"* as the first strategy.)

<hr>

——————— Life Skills Connection ———————

Identifying and using key words to focus your thoughts is a strategy you can use for other school assignments. At school, most assignments have parts that specifically state or suggest how to effectively do the assignment. This is true in science, social studies, foreign language, or career technology class-rooms. At work, you may be required to complete forms that require written responses. These questions on these forms also contain key words that state the expectations for a response.

What other real-life connections can you suggest to help your students see the relevance of this game strategy?

• • •

<hr>

GAME STRATEGY: IDENTIFY READY-MADE STORIES AND IDEAS—REMEMBER WITH YOUR LEFT HAND

Effective test takers do not know what the on-demand prompt will be about before they open their test booklet, but they do not go into a test empty-handed. If they are familiar with the prompt format, they know the consistent parts and the expectations of a scorer. They know what kinds of topics they might write about, and the genres and lengths or organizations they might use to write a response.

This knowledge prepares students for the one-two punch—taking two hands to the test and using them as tools to remember. This strategy teaches students to use their left hand as a memory aid and take ready-made stories from their lives or ideas from reading or classroom study to the test. The next game strategy completes the one-two punch and teaches students to plan across their right hand in order to plan a focused, organized, and detailed response before they begin. Together these strategies reduce the students' fear of the blank page and provide students with "handy" tools to get started and be successful.

In this lesson, students will learn how to prepare and use a handful of ideas, topics, or stories that might be used for any prompt and to identify the most effective response for this prompt.

Game Plan Practice Session

Identify Ready-Made Stories and Ideas—Remember With Your Left Hand

Equipment	• Released writing to a prompt questions (use prompts previously studied to generate ready-made stories and use a new prompt for the does-this-work test) • Game plan books • Chart paper and markers
Connection	Test takers, as we looked at the predictable format of the prompts, we identified the key words that stated or suggested the topics and length or organization of a response. As you worked alone and in partners, these key words helped you focus the purpose of a response. As you lifted these key words out of the prompt, you wrote a focused sentence to state the purpose. Now are you ready for the one-two punch to knock out prompt writing? This is the strategy to give your writing power. Any sports team practices plays. They have these plays memorized so that the day of the game, they do not have to invent a play. Instead they use the preplanned plays they know will be successful. Like athletes, writers write about the same topic over and over. They use a good idea or story and write about it in different ways.
Game strategy: Teaching point	You do not have to wait until the day you take the test to decide what to write about. Sure, you might not know the topic of the prompt until you open your test booklet, but you know a lot about the types of prompts and topics you might face. You can actually go to the test with a handful of ideas and stories to write about. Let's pause for a second and make a quick list of the things you have already written for class assignments. (Collaboratively create a chart listing the topics of stories, personal writing, ideas, or reports assigned as class projects.) This is a great list, but what about the topics, ideas, and stories you have written on your own, or unfinished writing that is in your writer's notebook, or stories that you tell your friends over and over. (Make a personal list of these stories. Give each story a memorable title. Titles make it easier to remember a story. Model creating titles by telling a personal story. Then ask them to think of a personal story and title it. The titles might name the setting [*Silverton Café*], problem [*Bicycle Crash*], key action [*Fighting Back*], or important people [*Dad's Suit*].) These important ideas or stories, even if they are about ordinary events, might be ready-made ideas and stories usable on a test. So let's see if you can fill up one hand with ready-made ideas and stories that might be usable the day you take the test. Let me show you how this works. Review key words from a prompt. Raise your left hand and think aloud a list of ready-made ideas and stories connected to this prompt and your text expectation. For example, if your test requires personal narrative, think of an ordinary story about a daily event that could have happened to your students or an important event that happened to someone else, possibly a current event or a historical event they remember in detail. Many times, students do not think ordinary events can be used on a test. For example, attending a birthday party can be used to show caring, responsibility, happiness, conflict, or persistence. Create a title for each story that captures the main idea of the event and makes it easy to remember the story, such as *Bullies on the Playground, The Tallest Roller Coaster*, or *The Apology*. Students need to see that connection to the prompt, a solid organization, and rich detail will make any ordinary story an excellent choice. Consider events students have studied in social studies or science if they know the details and can write about the event or idea in a rich way. Put each story or idea on a finger of your left hand. As you do, give a very brief summary of the story or idea and title it with a memorable title.)

Skill practice: Try it in partnerships	(Use an overhead or create and distribute a student handout of Identify Ready-Made Stories and Ideas, available as Figure 5.2. Encourage students to use their hands and touch their fingers in the same way you did when you modeled. Touching each finger increases future and effective use of this memory strategy.) So it is your turn to try filling up a hand with ready-made stories and ideas. The process I just used is listed for you on the overhead (or handout). Take five minutes to identify a handful of stories and ideas that you know something about and could use on a test. Try to get two to three ideas or stories on your left hand. I'll tell you when it is time to turn and share your list with a partner.
	Now it's time to share the stories and ideas you have identified and put on your left hand to create the first part of that power-punch. You will only have six minutes to share, so focus your stories and ideas so you can tell them in a brief summary. (Listen to students as they work in partnerships and gather some ideas they are putting on their hands. Report those ideas to the whole class to save time so you can move quickly to the next teaching point. Be sure to use a title for these stories that sounds memorable and remind students that titling stories makes them memorable.)
	How many of you just thought of a new idea or story as you talked? How many of you thought of a new idea listening to your partner? Pull out your game plan books and start a new entry. Write "Important, Ready-Made Stories and Ideas I Know" at the top of the page. Then list the stories and ideas you have on your hand so far.
Game strategy: Teaching point	Great work. Now, we have this handful of stories and ideas. (Distribute a clean, unmarked prompt to students. Give students a moment to reread and underline, highlight or circle the key words that focus their planning decisions.) Now let's see how this strategy helps you when you take the test. I will use the does-this-work-test on my handful of stories or ideas (adjust your language based on the length or organization expectations of your prompt) using the first prompt we read yesterday. I need to read the prompt again to remind myself of the key words. Then I'll ask, "Do I have an idea or story that I can use in my response?" Yesterday I had to generate a list of ideas and stories, but today, I have a handful of ready-made stories and ideas to use. I just need to check my list and see if any of these stories fit. (Take the first prompt from yesterday, put it on the overhead, and do the does-this-work test (see Figure 5.3 on page 98) on each of the stories and ideas on your hand. Finally, select the single response that you believe will turn into the best response. Explain why.)
Own it: Independent practice	Now, it is your turn to try this with your handful of stories (or ideas) starting with a new prompt. Use this process. First, read and identify the key words from the prompt. Second, take the does-this-work test to see if any stories or ideas you have already identified will fit this prompt. Third, identify one or two new stories or ideas that could also fit this prompt. Write these in your game plan book. Last, select the story or idea that best fits the prompt.
	(As students work, remind them to use their hands to remember their lists and to add new stories and ideas to their lists. Help students think aloud by listening to their stories. Remind them to create memorable titles.)

(Continued)

(Continued)

Huddle: Assess and reflect	How many of your stories and ideas could you use for prompt 1? Or prompt 2? Are there stories that fit one prompt and not the other? Are there stories or ideas you want to add to your list of ready-made stories and ideas after listening to a teammate? Take a moment and add to your list now.
Review game strategy: Link	Remember: writers find a way to use a good story several times or write about a good idea in several ways. In the same way, test takers come prepared knowing they have important, ready-made stories and ideas. Coming to the test with a handful of stories on your left hand that might be used for a variety of prompts is essential for a test taker's one-two punch.
Closing the session	(In their game plan books, have students record notes about this strategy in their own words. If you are charting, add "*Identifying ready-made stories and ideas*" and "*Using the does-this-work test*" to the "Writing to a Prompt Game Strategies" chart.)

Figure 5.2   Identify Ready-Made Stories and Ideas

Step 1: Identify the key words in a test prompt.

Step 2: List stories on your left hand that might fit the prompt.
- Stories I have told or written before
- Stories about me
- Stories about people I know
- Stories about people I have read about

Step 3: Title the stories.

Figure 5.3   Does-This-Work Test

Step 1: Identify the key words from a test prompt. Using key words, write a sentence to focus your purpose.

Step 2: Identify your favorite story or idea on your left hand.
- How does the story fit the prompt?
- What details make it fit the prompt?
- What details would you add, cut, or change to make it fit?

Step 3: Use the same process to check other stories or ideas on your left hand. Which one fits best?

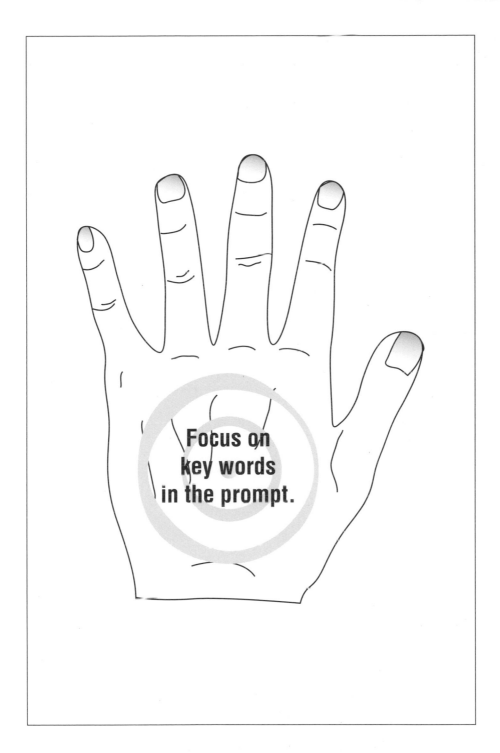

Focus on
key words
in the prompt.

Life Skills Connection

Being prepared often is simply anticipating the possible prompts or challenges you might face and having an answer ready. There are lots of times in life that ready-made answers save you from making mistakes or being confused.

Examples

- At work, you will probably be trained to respond to customer complaints or special requests. Having a ready-made answer for common complaints and requests makes your company look efficient and customer-friendly.
- At home, your family may have given you instructions on how to handle phone calls when they are not at home. If you babysit, you learn the ready-made responses to phone calls as part of your job.

    What other real-life connections can you suggest to help your students see the relevance of this game strategy?

● ● ●

GAME STRATEGY: PAUSE TO PLAN—PLAN ACROSS YOUR RIGHT HAND

Once test takers have decided on a single effective response, they must pause to plan. Like a time-out in basketball, planning and organizing before students write will ensure execution of a great play. Pausing to plan is that mental time-out to get it all together before stepping onto the court.

Two structures (narrative—personal and fictional—and expository or informative) are required most often for writing prompted questions. This lesson is best focused on the structure your students will use as they write the response. See Figure 5.1 on page 92 to decide what structure your students will use. The following is a basic game plan for pausing to plan.

Planning a Narrative

Narrative writing has essential elements. Whether the narrative is personal or fictional, knowing these essential elements and how to use them enables students to write effectively in a test setting. If your students studied, crafted, revised, and finished narratives over weeks in your classroom, these essential elements have become decisions that can easily transfer to an on-demand prompt.

Teaching students a planning strategy focuses this extensive work and reminds them of the decisions that transfer most easily to test writing. A test response requires a narrative focused on illustrating a central idea and staying on topic. As a result, keep planning simple and focused on the few things that will improve a score. Focus on the central idea, sequence, actions, and details that show the response's purpose. In more artful narratives, small digressions might add depth to a story. On a test, effective narratives have focus, sequence, specific details, and engaging craft that support the narrative's purpose, like dialogue, thoughts, and passages of description. Because most test narratives are head-to-pen drafts, students must plan the writing and then write it with a high degree of quality. The process is compressed because the time is compressed. (Check your rubric to identify the qualities of a narrative required by your state test and if students will have time to revise or edit their work.)

Figure 5.4   Plan a Narrative Across Your Right Hand

Narrative Steps

Step 1: Use the key words from the prompt to select an appropriate story from your handful of ready-made stories. Use the does-this-work test to determine the most important part of the story. Focus the key events of the narrative to ensure it connects to the prompt.

Step 2: Write a lead that states the focus of the narrative.

Step 3: Identify the beginning of the story. Plan across your fingers identifying key actions and details. Use words like *first*, *next*, *then*, *after*, and *finally* to help you remember the actions and details in sequential order. Identify the action that started the story, the actions that occurred in the middle, and the action that ended the story.

Step 4: Identify the description, thoughts, feelings, and dialogue that show how the narrative illustrates the prompt. Retell the story across your fingers adding these interesting details that show how the actions affected people in the story and why the story is important to tell.

Step 5: Write an ending that restates your purpose for telling the narrative or makes a comment on the story. You may want to explicitly connect your narrative to the prompt by repeating key words.

NOTE: Students with more sophisticated or stylistic writing will go beyond this basic planning process and crafting decisions.

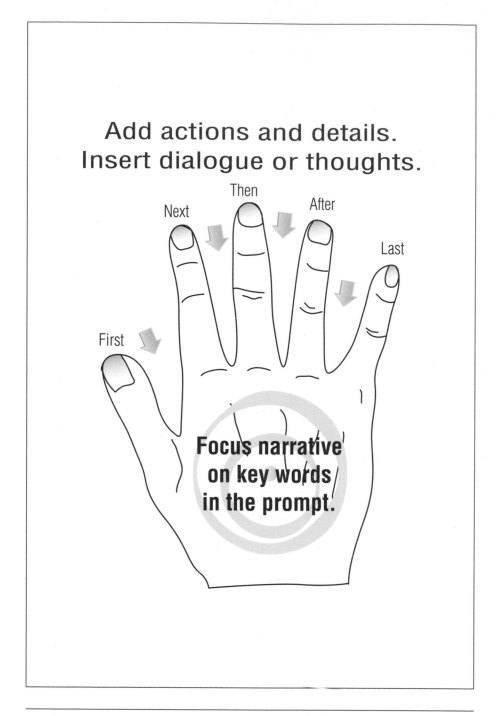

Add actions and details.
Insert dialogue or thoughts.

Then

Next

After

Last

First

Focus narrative on key words in the prompt.

Figure 5.5   Transition Words and Phrases for Sequencing Personal Narratives

Narrative Transitions		
Beginning	*Middle*	*End*
at first, first, in the first place	after, as soon as, before, eventually, later, next, then, in the meantime, soon	at last, finally, last

Planning Expository or Informative Responses

Students can use many of the decisions they made as they wrote and revised expository or informative essays in your classroom. This strategy focuses the more in-depth work you have previously taught and reminds students of the pieces that transfer most easily to test writing. However, a test response requires an essay written in a single session. Often, younger students use a more formulaic frame to keep them focused. Depending on your state rubric, a formulaic frame may be both helpful and acceptable for achieving success. (Check your rubric to identify the qualities of essays required by your state test.)

Whether students are writing a single paragraph or five paragraphs, the key to this structure is a well-stated claim or thesis. This claim is the central idea from the prompt and the focus for the response. Students will illustrate, explain, or describe the claim with parallel points. They will use a main point and supporting details for each point in the essay. Thinking through the claim is key for this type of essay. Keep planning simple and focused on the few things that will improve a score. Focus on the claim or central idea, organization, and details that illustrate and support the purpose of the response. If your students have written on historical events, important people, or core democratic values, remind them that these reports give them detailed knowledge that can be used on some test prompts.

Figure 5.6

Step 1: Use the key words from the prompt to select an appropriate idea from your handful of ready-made ideas. Use the does-this-work test to determine the most effective idea. Write a claim or thesis statement to focus your purpose and connect to the prompt.

Step 2: Write the sentence that states the claim using key words from the prompt. A two-sentence claim that explains the purpose of your paragraph or essay might be more effective.

Step 3: Focus the essay by identifying, two or three times, facts, reasons, or examples that illustrate your claim. Plan across your hand creating an order for the main points (examples or facts) that illustrate your claim. The order of the points shows the relationship or order of the content.

Step 4: Expand each important example or fact by adding specific supporting details. Reasons and explanation increase the reader's understanding of your purpose and connect your examples to the prompt.

Step 5: Write an ending that restates your purpose or makes a comment. You may want to explicitly connect your paragraph or essay to the prompt by repeating key words from the prompt.

NOTE: More sophisticated organizations or stylistic writing decisions will go beyond this basic planning process.

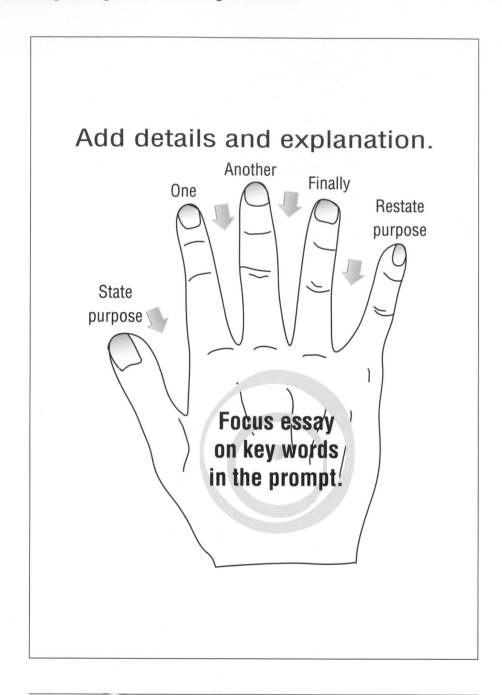

Figure 5.7 Transition Words and Phrases for Ordering Expository or Informative Essays

Transitions	
Time	*Importance*
after, as soon as, at first, then, at last/finally, before, in the first place, in the meantime, later, next, soon	additionally, again, also, and, as well, besides, equally important, further, furthermore, in addition, moreover, then

Game Plan Practice Session

Pausing to Plan—Plan Across Your Right Hand

Equipment	• Released writing to a prompt questions (use prompts studied in class) • Game plan books • Chart paper and markers
Connection	Test takers, are you ready for the second part of the one-two punch to knock out prompt writing? You already know how to prepare ready-made stories and ideas for the test. You came to class today with your left hand filled with stories and ideas. Plus you know that you might add or change details in these stories so they fit the prompt. Now you will pause to plan before you write. You will use your right hand for planning. Test takers who pause to plan write more successfully than writers who just start writing.
Game strategy: Teaching point	Begin this work by reviewing a prompt we have studied before. Select the key words and identify a story or idea on your left hand that fits this prompt. If you cannot find a story or idea, create a new one. Add this story or idea to your left hand and to your list in your game plan books. Use a prompt that students have previously studied. Read and review or give them time to become familiar with the prompt. Be sure each student has a story or idea before you begin teaching the class how and why to use the right hand for planning. Now let me show you how to plan across your right hand. Planning across your right hand organizes your response and helps you remember specific details to make the writing interesting and complete. (Model planning across your right hand using the organizational structure, either narrative or expository, required for your test. See Figures 5.4 [page 101], 5.5, 5.6 [page 103], and 5.7 [above]. Think aloud your plan using the steps for each structure.)

(Continued)

(Continued)

Skill practice: Try it in partnerships	(In partnerships, students take turns thinking aloud to plan and rehearse a story or idea from their own ready-made stories and ideas.) NOTE: You may elect to break this game plan session into two parts: Part 1: Oral practice of the planning. Part 2: Written practice of the planning.
Own it: Independent practice	Today, as you write a response, write slowly. Pause after you write about each finger of your plan. Reread your response to be sure that you are including all the details you told your partner. Sometimes we tell stories with more details than when we write them. Stopping to reread or stopping to check your hand also reminds you to put all those great details on the page. (Independently, students write the story or idea they just rehearsed. Stop at student desks to check on their progress. Compliment them as they work and point out the behaviors that will make a difference: rereading, stopping to revisit the plan, touching fingers to remember the plan, etc.)
Huddle: Assess and reflect	(Ask students to reread their writing to find evidence of their planning. Look for evidence of key words from the prompt, organization, and specific details for the content of the response.)
Review game strategy: Link	Pausing to plan provides time to ensure you answer the prompt in the prompt, organize your writing, and provide sufficient details to illustrate your thinking.
Closing the session	(In their game plan books, have students self-assess their planning. Did they use the time effectively? On what step in the process do they need to spend more time? How might they return to their planning hand as they write to ensure they get their great thinking on paper? If you are charting, add *"Pausing to plan—plan across your right hand"* to the "Writing to a Prompt Game Strategies" chart.)

Life Skills Connection

Using your hand to plan gives you a structure to attach the sequence of events or order of ideas in a paper. Your hand is a way to remember a process. In some ways it is like a mnemonic.

Mnemonics are an easy way to remember facts for school. You might use the word *homes* to remember the five great lakes: Huron, Ontario, Michigan, Erie, and Superior. However, many people create mnemonics to remember personal information. I use my first dog's name to remember my garage door password (Otto translates to five, seven, seven, five on the keypad).

What other real-life connections can you suggest to help your students see the relevance of this game strategy?

• • •

GAME STRATEGY: WRITE SLOWLY AND CONSCIOUSLY

The final game strategy raises the quality of test writing, but it is a mindset that raises the quality of all writing. A test is not the time to freewrite, fast write, or quick write. Your students have just carefully planned. Now is the time to write a slow, conscious, quality response. Quality on-demand writing is best achieved with slow and conscious writing that revisits the plan. Test takers know a reader (scorer) is going to score the writing; therefore, they slow down, reread, rethink, and revise as they write in order to make sense and connect to a reader (scorer).

Game Plan Practice Session

Writing Slowly and Consciously

Equipment	• Released writing to a prompt questions (use a new prompt students have not previously studied) • Paper for a response. If your state releases the paper identical to the paper in the test booklet, copy it. This gives students a sense of an implicit length so they do not write too little or too much. • Game plan books • Chart paper and markers
Connection	You are ready for this test. You know the format and expectations. You know the one-two punch with your list of ready-made stories and ideas and your pause to plan across your hand. The only thing left to do is write. But writing for a test takes conscious thinking. So you will write slowly, paying attention. You will stop, reread, and maybe even revise as you write. Writing slowly and consciously will help you maintain your focus and use everything you know about good writing. (If your test is timed, encourage students to plan for the first five minutes and then pace their writing time to ensure an effective and complete response.)
Game strategy: Teaching point	Today, you will write from a new prompt. You will apply all your strategies. (Review the list of strategies on the chart.) However, as you write, you will practice writing slowly and consciously.
Skill practice: Try it in partnerships	(There is no skill practice in this lesson. Students will be writing in a test setting to practice the mindset of writing slowly and consciously.)
Own it: Independent practice	Students, read the prompt, lift key words, use the one-two punch as you use your left hand to review your list of ready-made stories and ideas and select one story or idea. When you are finished planning across your right hand, slowly and consciously write your response. (Watch as your students plan across their fingers and write. Remind them to return to their planning—touching their fingers to remember the plan—as they write so they can stay focused and on topic and include their purposeful planning in the response.)

(Continued)

(Continued)

Huddle: Assess and reflect	(After writing, ask students to create a "Things I Did" chart in the game plan books. Ask them to quickly list the things they did as they read the prompt and wrote their response.

Things I Did as I Read	Things I Did as I Wrote

Review game strategy: Link	Test takers are conscious of the strategies they use as they read a prompt and write an answer. Writing slowly and consciously raises the quality of the writing and the score.
Closing the session	(In their game plan books, have students reread the list of strategies they used and the strategies they know how to use. Ask them to self-assess their test sense. What did they do that they want to do next time? What did they do that they want to avoid doing next time? If you are charting, add *"Writing slowly and consciously"* to the "Writing to a Prompt Game Strategies" chart.)

─────────────── **Life Skills Connection** ───────────────

Effective test takers are confident. They know what to do and how to do it because they understand the test. Having test sense makes all the difference because test takers can go slowly and think about making adjustments as they take the test. Confidence is a bonus advantage earned from strategy-based preparation.

Examples

- In sports, players know how to behave under pressure. A quarterback knows to whom to throw the ball after the snap because he has called the play.
- At work, you might face a challenging emergency, but your company has trained you how to act in a tornado or if someone falls. You have the knowledge to act quickly and safely.

What other real-life connections can you suggest to help your students see the relevance of this game strategy?

─────────────── • • • ───────────────

> ### Writing to a Prompt Game Strategies
>
> - Identify the topic and structure—lift key words
> - Identify ready-made stories and ideas—remember with your left hand
>   - Use the does-this-work test
>   - Does the story or idea fit the prompt?
>   - How is it a good example of the prompt?
>   - What details can I use to make it work?
>
> - Pause to plan—plan across your right hand
> - Write slowly and consciously

ASSESSMENT

The four strategies in this chapter on writing to a prompt construct knowledge about how the test works and how writers can focus and use what they already know to write for a test. As you assess your students, look for several behaviors: (1) During independent planning and writing, students use the strategies: highlighting or underlining key words in the prompt, using both hands to remember or plan, writing slowly and pausing to reread and consciously write a response. (2) During teammate conversations and self-assessment, students explain their process, plan, or writing decisions to teammates. Combine observation of your students' actions and talk with their pen and paper performances to identify a focused "next step" rather than to fix everything at once. In a test-preparation unit, small moves can be accomplished that can have a large impact on student performance. Creating a metacognitive awareness of what to expect and what process to use makes the biggest difference. Do the following things to identify the next single teaching point or the next single writing goal:

1. Sort papers quickly for one quality. One approach to quickly sort and assess papers is provided below. Narrative or expository essays can be quickly sorted into three stacks that provide insight into a next teaching point. For example, if you find that most of your students are summarizing a story, listing the actions in sequence, the next teaching point might be to encourage them to focus on the most important part of the story. Once that focus is identified, it is easier for them to see the beginning, middle, and end of the story and why a series of actions with details help a reader understand the point they are trying to make. Use student samples to show how to think through raising the quality of their next writing and "bump" their writing simply by improving their organization. Be aware that more sophisticated organizations have more sophisticated qualities of good writing.

Personal Narrative	Expository/Information
(1) List	(1) List

(2) Sense of story
• Chronological sequence
• Details
	(2) Clearly stated answer
	   • Two to three points to explain or illustrate the answer
	   • Details to explain the points

(3) Story focused on an important moment
• Clear beginning, middle, and end
• Chronological sequence
• Actions and details
	(3) Clearly stated claim with points and details: times, kinds, facts, reasons, or examples
	   • Transitions at the beginning of paragraphs show relationship of points
	   • Major details explain each point
	   • Specific minor details explain or illustrate how and why the major details are important to understand

2. Confer with students. Listen to students' explanations of what they are consciously doing as you review their pen and paper performance. Identify the strengths in both thinking and writing and compliment them. Suggest a single strategy or tip to improve the quality of each student's writing or thinking. Imagine it goes like this: *I see, you are trying to do "this."* (Rephrase what the student explained.) *And when you transfer that from your head to the page, this is the result. Plus you are doing " this" very well.* (Name something and point to words on the page.) *Nice job. Now let me suggest one thing that you can try the next time you write to raise the quality of your test writing.*

3. Using the state rubric, have students identify the key qualities of successful prompt writing. Using this focused list from your state rubric, have students score their responses looking for evidence in their writing that they used from the qualities on the list. (For Grades 3 and 4, reduce the qualities on the list.)

4. Self-check. Have students self-check what they know and what they use to identify a personal goal for the next time they write (see Figure 5.8).

Figure 5.8   Writing to a Prompt Self-Check

	What I Know	*What I Used*
• Identify the topic and organization—lift key words		
• Identify ready-made stories and ideas I know		

• Use the does-this-work test
  o Does the story or idea fit the prompt?
  o How is it a good example of the prompt?
  o What details can I use to make it work?		

• Pause to plan—plan across your right hand		
• Write slowly and consciously		
Personal Goal:		

FINAL THOUGHTS

Reduce and focus your teaching during test preparation just prior to a test experience. It is too late to teach everything your students need to know. Instead engage in a few focused reading or writing strategies that translate to improved scores. These few focused strategies are the "cheat-codes" that gamers use or the plays football players learn. You have the rest of the year to engage in quality teaching and learning that translates to successful test performance.

Become a test expert. To focus your teaching, study your state test. Pay attention to your thinking as you analyze writing to a prompt questions as well as when you plan and then write your own responses. As the test expert, your students count on you to coach them on game sense or test sense. Test sense requires that you make your thinking visible so students can use your model or a teammate's model as a guide to their thinking on the test.

Preparing to Use This Unit of Study

6

A successful face-to-face team is more than just collectively intelligent. It makes everyone work harder, think smarter, and reach better conclusions than they would have on their own.

—James Surowiecki (2005, p. 27)

GAME STRATEGY FOR TEACHERS

Understand That . . .
- Professional learning communities tend to enhance planning, teaching, and learning.
- Administrative support is essential in creating change in schools and classrooms.

Know
- Preparation checklist for preparing a unit of study
- Fun ways to introduce a unit of study

Able to Do
- Meet with a partner or group to study your state test and plan lessons

PLANNING TIPS AND TOOLS

This final chapter includes tools to help you plan and ideas to support you as you prepare your unit of study.

Use a checklist to begin with the end in mind. Figure 6.1, Checklist: Preparing for the Test-Taking Unit of Study (page 117) is a general list of what we suggest you do to prepare for the unit. Note that we suggest looking over your state test with a study group or professional learning community. It has been our experience that the best teacher planning and preparation comes through collaboration with colleagues. In his book *Results Now* (2006), Mike Schmoker illustrates the value of teacher collaboration. In summarizing his research on the challenges faced by educators who teach in isolation, Schmoker notes, "Like no other profession, teachers are denied the opportunity to learn from our actions and our results" (p. 34). Working together with colleagues and using the ideas and checklists in this chapter will help you be more efficient and effective in planning and teaching this unit of study. Schmoker also notes that administrators are essential in helping support and encourage teachers in the collaboration process. The following are ways administrators can support teachers in preparing for and using this unit of study.

- Find ways to help teachers arrange time to plan together.
  o Find people to cover classes (e.g. administrators, substitutes, other teachers) so that teachers can spend time planning.
  o Use part of your professional development days for planning.
  o Use early or late start days for planning.
  o Support teachers who are using before-school, lunch, or after-school time to plan by
    – applying for them to get continuing credits for the time spent.
    – bringing them food and beverages!
    – helping them purchase materials needed.
  o Ask teachers who are experiencing success with their students to share at staff meetings so other teachers can be inspired and get ideas.
  o Meet with teachers to help them analyze their tests and plan the units.

In preparing to use the checklist, you will need to determine who is going to be a part of your study group or professional learning community (PLC) and when and where you will hold your first meeting. Since you will be studying your state test, don't plan the meeting date until you have gotten samples of your state test released items. You can find your state test released items at Assessment Resources and Released Items Curriculum Development (http://www.aea267.k12.ia.us/cia/math/ stateitems.html).

Once you have studied your tests and determined which lessons from the unit you will be teaching (See the Game Plan Overview Chart at the end of this chapter. This is a checklist of all of the lessons in the unit.) you will want to plan how to get started on the unit. (If you teach in upper grades, remember that the lessons in the unit can be divided up and taught among content area teachers. The work of this unit of study should not be left solely to the English teacher.) Included in this chapter are some fun ideas and suggestions for making learning to take tests fun and meaningful for you and your students.

IDEAS AND SUGGESTIONS FOR MAKING THE TEST-TAKING UNIT FUN!

- Create a bulletin board titled "Winning Strategies for Test Taking." Make it look like a football field, with a goal post. As students learn new strategies, have them add a strategy that moves them from one end of the field to the goal post. When they reach the goal (completing the unit of study). have a celebration for the new skills they learned.
- Have a Kick-Off Opening Day for the unit. Ask students to wear their favorite sports shirt or team colors. You wear yours.
  - Talk about why sports and games are so exciting and how the players learn strategies to help them improve. In this unit, they will be learning winning strategies to help them be strategic test takers.
  - Talk about team spirit and how everyone in this unit will be helping everyone else learn to be better test takers.
  - Talk about how the strategies they learn in playing sports can help them in life (being strategic, a team player, a good sport, etc.) and in this unit they will learn how strategies for taking tests will also help them in life outside of school. Include nonphysical, competitive games in your conversations. Remember some of your students play video games or other competitive games that require the same strategies and team-player mentalities as physical sports.
  - For fun, you can use a whistle and stopwatch as you do group management during the units.
- Read the book *Diffendoofer Day* by Dr. Seuss to your students. It's a great story and pep talk about teaching students how to think.

- Make up a team cheer that you chant at the beginning and end of each lesson.
  - o "Yes, we are the best! Yes, we can take tests. We are smarter than the rest—strategies help us know, not guess!"
  - o "Hail to the smart test takers, they have the skills to make it. Hail, hail to _____ (name of school), the best students in the land!" (This was modeled after the University of Michigan team song. You can make one up based on your own favorite team chant.)

CONCLUSION

We wrote this book to help make test-preparation manageable and fun for teachers and students. Test taking is important and has value in our schools, but remember that it is the day-to-day relationship you build with your students and the wonderful teaching practices you use with them all year long that will keep them inspired! You have the power to change lives. You have the power to create lifelong learners. You make a difference in the lives of young people. Go Team!

Figure 6.1   Checklist: Preparing for the Test-Taking Unit of Study

	Task	Who?	When?	Done
1.	Obtain examples of released tests or items from your state tests			
2.	In a study group or PLC, analyze the types of items and types of questions that are on your state's test (multiple choice, constructed response, writing prompts).			
3.	After analyzing the types of items and questions on your test, go thru the Game Plan Overview Chart (see Figure 6.2) and check the lessons (game plans) you think your students will need.			
4.	It's a great idea to have each teacher actually *take* the test. It will really help you understand the kind of thinking you need to do to take your state test.			
5.	Select several examples from your state released test of the types of questions that will be on the test to use in teaching the lessons. You can also use questions from your textbook to supplement if needed. With a teaching partner, write several think-alouds that you will insert into a game plan lesson.			
6.	Mark your calendars or lesson planners with dates when you will teach the lessons (see the end of this chapter for a blank monthly calendar).			
7.	Read Chapter 1 and be sure everyone in your study group or PLC understands what metacognition, modeling, think-alouds, and scaffolding are.			
8.	Gather materials or equipment you need to prepare for the units.			
9.	Decide how you are going to "kick off" the unit and get ready to get started.			
10.	Reflect: After teaching the unit and taking the test, meet and reflect with your study group or PLC and determine what worked and what you would do differently next year. When your scores are announced, analyze the data to focus your daily instruction and reevaluate your test-preparation unit of study.			

Figure 6.2   Game Plan Overview

Determine which lessons you will need to teach your students.		
Chapter 2: Test-Reading Strategies	**Yes**	**No**
Interacting and Distracting Voices		
Rereading		
Expository Text Structures		
Reading Graphics		
Narrative Text Structures		
Watching the Characters		
Chapter 3: Question-Answering Strategies	**Yes**	**No**
Understanding Questions That Have "Almost Right" Answers		
Understanding Questions That Use Facts From the Text as Wrong Answer Choices		
Understanding "Not" and "Except" Questions		
Understanding What the Questions Ask		
Chapter 4: Constructed Response Questions	**Yes**	**No**
Determining the Text Structure of a Question		
Knowing the Difference Between Literal and Inferential Responses		
Writing a Quality Response		
Memorize the RESCUE Strategy		
Chapter 5: Writing to a Prompt	**Yes**	**No**
Identify the Topic and Structure—Lift Key Words		
Identify Ready-Made Stories and Ideas—Remember With Your Left Hand		
Pause to Plan—Plan Across Your Right Hand		
Write Slowly and Consciously		

Figure 6.3   Test Unit Calendar

Month(s):				
Monday	*Tuesday*	*Wednesday*	*Thursday*	*Friday*
—	—	—	—	—
—	—	—	—	—
—	—	—	—	—
—	—	—	—	—
—	—	—	—	—

References

Anderson, C. (2005). *Assessing writers.* Portsmouth, NH: Heinemann.

Boynton, A., & Blevins, W. (2003). *Teaching students to read nonfiction.* New York: Scholastic.

Calkins, L. (2001). *The art of teaching reading.* New York: Addison-Wesley.

Calkins, L., Montgomery, K., Falk, B., & Santman, D. (1998). *A teacher's guide to standardized reading tests.* Portsmouth, NH: Heinemann.

Dickson, S. V., Simmons, D. C., & Kame'enui, E. J. (1998). Text organization: Research bases. In D. C. Simmons & E. J. Kame'enui (Eds.), *What reading research tells us about children with diverse learning needs* (pp. 239–278). Mahwah, NJ: Erlbaum.

Dymock, S. (2005). Teaching expository text structure awareness. *The Reading Teacher, 59*(2), 177–182.

Gallagher, K. (2004). *Deeper reading.* Portland, ME: Stenhouse.

Gee, J. P. (2003). *What video games have to teach us about learning and literacy.* New York: Palgrave Macmillan.

Gee, J. P. (2004). *Situated language and learning: A critique of traditional schooling.* New York: Routledge Taylor and Francis Group.

Gere, A. R., Christenbury, L., & Sassi, K. (2005). *Writing on demand: Best practices and strategies for success.* Portsmouth, NH: Heinemann.

Harvey, S., & Goudvis, A. (2007). *Strategies that work: Teaching comprehension for understanding and engagement* (2nd ed). Portland, ME: Stenhouse.

Johnston, P. (2004). *Choice words: How our language affects children's learning.* Portland, ME: Stenhouse.

Klem, A. M., & Connell, J. P. (2004). Relationships matter: Linking teacher support to student engagement and achievement. *Journal of School Health, 74*(7), 262–273.

Montelongo, J. A., & Hernandez, A. C. (2007). Reinforcing expository reading and writing skills: A more versatile sentence completion task. *The Reading Teacher, 60,* 538–546.

National Research Council. (2000). *How people learn: Brain, mind, experience, and school.* Washington, DC: National Academy Press.

Roser, N., Martinez, M., Fuhrken, C., & McDonald, K. (2007). Characters as guides to meaning. *The Reading Teacher, 60,* 548–559.

Schmoker, M. (2006). *Results now: How we can achieve unprecedented improvements in teaching and learning.* Alexandria, VA: Association for Supervision and Curriculum Development.

Surowiecki, J. (2005). *The wisdom of crowds: Why the many are smarter than the few and how collective wisdom shapes business, economies, societies and nations.* New York: Random House.

Tovani, C. (2000). *I read it, but I don't get it.* Portland, ME: Stenhouse.

Index